The Axial Ages of World History
Lessons for the 21st Century

Throughout human history, perhaps even pre-human, there has been a tension between the need for order and the forces that cause change. That tension is greater now than ever, because, in our increasingly globalized world, the rate of change is also increasing. This book finally explains how we can cope: we have stories. We live our narratives.

— Brian Spooner, University of Pennsylvania, is author of *Literacy in the Persianate World: Writing and the Social Order.*

The idea that Axial Ages occurred, and that they provide warnings/opportunities for us today, seems both new and useful. But the value of this book is additional to this stance, in that it looks at cultural change - civilizations - from a complexity viewpoint. These changes are certainly complicated, but the pressures are interwoven and therefore need to be understood as complex. The book does a good job of explaining our present cultural difficulties - our prospective emergencies social, ecological and physical - in a wholly new way. Perhaps we'll get new answers...

— Jack Cohen, evolutionary biologist, is coauthor of *The Collapse of Chaos*, with Ian Stewart.

This is a challenging and creative tour de force on comparative, global, world history and cross-cultural, complex societal dynamics. Without doubt one of the most stimulating works in the tradition of big history and macro analysis."

— Claudio Cioffi-Revilla, George Mason University, is author of *Power Laws in the Social Sciences: Discovering Non-equilibrium Dynamics in the Social Universe.*

The Axial Ages of World History
Lessons for the 21st Century

Ken Baskin
&
Dmitri M. Bondarenko

Cover art: Martha Aleo

The Axial Ages of World History: Lessons for the 21st Century
Written by: Ken Baskin & Dmitri M. Bondarenko

Library of Congress Control Number: 2014957277

ISBN: 978-1-938158-14-8

Copyright © 2014
Emergent Publications,
3810 N. 188th Ave, Litchfield Park, AZ 85340, USA

All rights reserved. No part of this publication may be reproduced, stored on a retrieval system, or transmitted, in any form or by any means, electronic, mechanical, photocopying, microfilming, recording or otherwise, without written permission from the publisher.

Printed in the United States of America

Dedication

We dedicate this book to the memories of our mothers, Victoria Rothman Baskin and Lidia Nikitichna Bondarenko, whose encouragement, support, and championing of the intellectual life enabled us to become the type of people who would write a book like this.

Contents

A note from the coauthors on the challenges of
this book xi
Challenge One: The balance between two equally
important audiences..xi
Challenge Two: The dangers of oversimplification
vs. our desire for a short book xii

Prologue..1
References 5

Chapter 1
The Axial Age as cultural transformation:
A dream of social order 7
Introduction.. 7
The Axial Age reconsidered 9
On stories 11
Initial conditions 15
Fragmentation 17
Foundational stories..21
Intensification of war 25
New world stories...28
Commentary on the world story....................................37
Empire emerges...39
References 40

Chapter 2
Modernity as a second Axial Age:
The dream of rational order 49
Introduction...49
Political fragmentation...52
Foundational story 53
Negotiating the new world story....................................58
Intensification of warfare...60
The new world story 64
Enlightenment commentary..68
Empire? 79
References 82

Chapter 3
Notes toward a Science 2.0 theory of human history 89
Introduction 89
On networks 92
Evolution 2.0 94
The pattern of evolving phenomena 98
Cultural Evolution 2.0 104
Some implications 115
References 119

Chapter 4
Redefining otherness for the 21st century 127
Conclusion 127
References 136

Acknowledgements

The ideas in this book dance across so many disciplinary boundaries that it was sometimes difficult to keep track of them. In the course of our explorations, we move from ancient history to molecular biology, from complexity sciences to philosophy. And that is only a sample of the many disciplines we incorporate. As a result, our acknowledgements should probably be very long or very short. So, like the book itself, we decided to keep it brief. We are extremely grateful for all the people whose writings and conversations have made important contributions to this book. But there are several whom we especially wanted to note.

Three sets of contributors stand out. First, several colleagues have inspired and provided direction for the ideas we have developed. While it is difficult to separate out a few from the many who have contributed so vitally to our thought, we wanted especially to single out Henri Claessen in cultural anthropology, Merlin Donald in cognitive neuroscience, Stanley Salthe in evolutionary theory, Jesper Hoffmeyer in biosemiotics, Jan Assmann in religious studies, Karl Jaspers and Schmuel Eisenstadt in the history of the Axial Age, David Boje in dynamic story theory, and Bruno Latour in actor-network theory.

A second set of people gave us the opportunity to discuss our ideas as they emerged, helping us determine which ideas opened pathways we wanted to explore and which we needed to avoid. Once again, of the many colleagues with whom we discussed these ideas, several provided especially vital insights—evolutionary biologist Jack

Cohen, historians Leonid Grinin and Andrey Korotayev, and anthropologist Brian Spooner.

Finally, we received a variety of types of support that proved essential in writing the book. Our publisher, Kurt Richardson, for example, has consistently—and very patiently—encouraged us from the beginnings of our work together. There have also been several people who, in addition to those with whom we've discussed our ideas, have given us valuable feedback as we wrote the book. Most importantly, we want to acknowledge Gary Floam, Tom Turner, and Martha Aleo.

To all these and the many, many more whose thoughts and assistance have made this book possible, we extend our deepest thanks.

A note from the coauthors on the challenges of this book

From the time we started talking about writing this book, we realized that we'd be facing two important challenges. We wanted to explain how we resolved those challenges so that you, our readers, can better understand why we wrote the book the way we did.

Challenge One: The balance between two equally important audiences

At first, the subject of this book—comparing the transformation of societies in Axial Age Greece, Israel, India, and China to the one in the modern era—seemed mostly of interest to academics. Yet, the more we talked about it, the more we came to believe that it might even be more important to the wider audience. That audience includes anyone trying to understand what is happening in the first quarter of the 21st century. The rapid growth of population, the advances in technology, the frightening intensity of warfare, the intensification of trade and the growing social inequality of both periods suggested a similarity that might be extremely valuable to both audiences.

As a result, we decided to write this book for both academic and non-academic audiences. This kind of balancing act required that we resist the temptation to use a lot of technical language. In some cases, we have probably followed Oscar Wilde's observation that the only way to get rid of temptation is to give in to it.

But for the most part we have, we hope, made our own observations as clearly and as accessibly as we could.

The double audience also made it important to note our sources without creating obstacles to non-academic readers. To do that, we note our sources in the text with the author's name, date of publication, and page number in parenthesis. Some non-academic readers may want to ignore those citations. But anyone who wants to explore more deeply has the sources. We also didn't want to overwhelm readers with too many sources. So, in some cases, we've indicated a larger body of writings with just two or three sources. Finally, when we thought a good number of readers might be interested in examining a topic further, we expanded the note and pointed to the best source or sources for that examination.

Challenge Two: The dangers of oversimplification vs. our desire for a short book

In this book, we treat a series of ideas that are either very new or known only to small audiences. In addition, our approach is deeply trans-disciplinary, drawing on fields ranging from ancient and modern history to neurobiology, complexity sciences to both cultural and evolutionary anthropology, from sociology to evolutionary biology and biosemiotics. To treat all these issues with the fullness they deserve would have required a much longer book. Yet, because so many of the ideas that we synthesized from these many disciplines are so new—and we want feedback from our readers—we decided to keep this book short, more a monograph than a full-length work.

As a result, we have consistently oversimplified our discussions where it seemed reasonable. We have, for instance, barely discussed the Axial Age transformations in Israel and India, and have presented our ideas on evolutionary "thickness" in a way that is more suggestive than comprehensive. In the end, we gave our readers a broad-brush treatment of a series of ideas we hope to develop in more detail at a later date. In the meantime, if our readers tell us that these ideas are misleading or confusing, we can make the appropriate mid-course corrections.

Our overriding purpose here is to offer you the outline of a different way of thinking about what is happening in the world today, through a better understanding of the past. History—we believe—is not "repeating" itself. But it seems to be following a pattern that has occurred before.

We hope you will agree that our insights are as valuable and provocative as we have found them.

Prologue

We are indeed approaching a culmination of sorts; our species seems to face a kind of test toward which basic forces of history have been moving us for millennia. It is a test of political imagination – of our ability to accept basic, necessary changes in the structures of governance – but also a test of moral imagination.[1]

— Robert Wright, *Nonzero*

As we write these words in 2014, political and financial leaders across the globe seem to have lost control of the societies they govern. In America, the most powerful and wealthiest nation on the planet has only recently discovered that it can pass a budget without a fiscal knife to its neck; its "top secrets" are openly discussed in the international press. China's growing wealth comes hand in hand with an epidemic of corruption, frequent riots, increasingly dangerous levels of pollution, and widespread anger among its minorities. An uneasy calm in European markets belies profound differences in culture and economic policy across the European Union. Riots in Ukraine drove its president from office, in spite, or perhaps because of Russian support, and have now brought the country to the brink of civil war. In Syria, another civil war continues to tear that country apart. The Egyptian military convicted three Al-Jazeera journalists with no real evidence and appears to have betrayed the nation's Arab Spring hopes for democracy, electing General El-Sisi its President. And a resolution to the Israeli-Palestinian standoff seems increasingly unlikely, as Israel and Hamas in Gaza seem on the brink of war.

Even more upsetting, these same leaders face a series of challenges in coming years that none is prepared to address. Climate change and ecological spoliation, competition for limited food, water, and energy resources, nuclear proliferation, and terrorism – all these and many other looming issues demand more international coordination than the governments of the world can currently exercise[2]. The inability to address any of this sampling of the world's challenges suggests that what we are experiencing is more than a random series of shocks. Something very basic in our governing institutions seems broken, and no one knows how to fix it. The only thing that is clear is the need to change the way nations cooperate, while how to do it effectively remains a mystery.

However, this is not the first such period in human history. Between 1000 and 800 BCE, several advanced societies across Eurasia – from Greece to India and China – found themselves unable to respond to the challenges of advancing technology, increasing wealth, and intensified warfare. The result was the period Karl Jaspers called the Axial Age (c. 800-200 BCE)[3]. In this book, we want to examine Modernity (c. 1500 CE-the present) as a second axial age. The similarities are striking: Just as advancing literacy transformed the axial world, the printing press transformed the modern world; as iron reinvented axial manufacture and warfare, the machine did the same for moderns; and the modern experiments in democracy and totalitarianism, capitalism and nationalism served the same purpose as the social experiments in democracy and advanced bureaucratic government, socio-economic systems and identity building of the Axial Age societies. All those experiments would unfold in both periods, as people relearned how to govern themselves in an increasingly complex social world that demanded they develop a different set of rules.

Our purpose in this short book is threefold: First, we want to examine the Axial Age and Modernity as thoroughgoing, transformational periods of crisis in world history. Second, we want to suggest a theory of cultural evolution that helps explain these periods. Third, we want to consider what the similarities between these periods suggest about addressing the problems that face societies across the planet today.

In pursuing this purpose, our first chapter will examine the transformation, during the Axial Age, from bronze-age cultures with mythic religions, governed by "divine" kings and their loyalty lineages, to iron-age cultures, with universalistic, ethical "Religions of the Book," governed by vast bureaucracies. The second chapter will turn to Modernity and its efforts to define ways of thinking and social institutions capable of governing an increasingly globalized world. For us, such globalization is not merely a contemporary, essentially economic process. Rather, the world is now experiencing the culmination of a process of intercultural interaction, immanent in world history, that has moved toward a global "federation" of local civilizations. In the third chapter, we offer a theory of cultural evolution to explain how a race of animals that must learn *everything* was able to expand from as few as 10,000 members in Africa about 70,000 years ago[4] to the dominant species in almost every environment on our planet. Finally, a brief conclusion considers what our approach suggests about the challenges and decisions people all over our globe face today.

We present these ideas as what Foucault calls "game openings" so that "those who may be interested are invited to join in"[5(224)]. The analysis we present is clearly oversimplified. We do not present a thorough examination of the many questions our approach opens. Rather, we hope the reader will find this approach as provocative and worth pursuing as we have.

With that in mind, we turn to the great transformation of the Axial Age, which witnessed the birth of modern warfare, the process by which literacy transformed human consciousness, the rise of universalistic, ethical religions, and governments' use of those religions as a form of social control.

References

1. Wright, R. (2000). Nonzero: The Logic of Human Destiny, New York: Vintage Books.
2. Sachs, J.D. (2008). Common Wealth: Economics for a Crowded Planet, New York: Penguin Press.
3. Jaspers, K. (1953). The Origins and Goal of History, Bullock, M. (trans.), New Haven, CT and London: Yale University Press.
4. Fagan, B.M. (2010). Cro-Magnon: How the Ice Age Gave Birth to the First Modern Humans, New York: Bloomsbury Press.
5. Foucault, M. (1994). "Questions of Method," in J.D. Faubion (ed.), Power, New York, NY: The New Press, pp. 223-38.

Chapter 1

The Axial Age as cultural transformation

A dream of social order

Introduction

> *[With the] new theory and practice of battle ... it was no longer killing in the service of the ancestors, but rather the organization of control of men in the service of the territorial prince that gave meaning to warfare.*[1]
>
> — Mark Lewis, *Sanctioned Violence in Early China*

From about 3000 to 1000 BCE, the most developed societies, from Egypt and Mesopotamia to India and China, governed very different cultures with similar social institutions. Agricultural surpluses were collected and distributed by central governments based in their mythological religions. (Greece, as we'll see, was an exception.) People in these societies believed that their kings had special connections to the gods or ancestors, and the kings were therefore responsible for the rituals that kept society ordered and prosperous. These kings governed by relying on the loyalty of an aristocratic class. War was mostly an exercise in aristocratic honor, a lot like what Homer shows in the *Iliad*.

Throughout this period, the successes of these societies led to major changes:

- Population grew, as the largest cities more than tripled from 40,000 in 3000 BCE to 150,000 in 1200 BCE[2(22,34)];

- Technology advanced, as the use of iron tools and weapons began to spread about 1200 BCE and horses and wheeled vehicles started being used in war about the same time[3];

- Trade between political entities – and the amount of wealth overall – also intensified starting about 1500 BCE[4].

By 1200 BCE, this change began to overwhelm many of these societies. In the Eastern Mediterranean area, states from the Aegean through the Fertile Crescent and Egypt had become an interdependent economic system[5]. Then, a series of shocks, probably including a climate shift and internal rebellions, led to a collapse of this system. As a result, many of the powers in this area – Mycenae in Greece, the Hittites in Turkey, Ugarit in Syria – collapsed. Egypt survived attacks by the "Sea People," as they called them, populations that may have been migrating from states that had collapsed, but Egypt would never be a world power again[6]. In China, the Zhou Dynasty would expand through the 10th century BCE, but fall apart in the 9th. Eventually, 170 independent kingdoms emerged[7]. The successes of these societies had changed their world so much that they needed a new set of social survival strategies.

The Axial Age reconsidered

Karl Jaspers[8(1)] characterized the period (c. 800-200 BCE) in which those new strategies emerged, as the "Axial Age," the "axis in world history ... which has given birth" to everything that followed. Jaspers and his school of thought explains the similar experiences in Greece and Israel, India and China largely in terms of their spiritual transformations. For him, these transformations happened unpredictably in these weakly connected, very different cultures[9,10,11,12,13]. However, for Jaspers, "The Axial period too ended in failure"[8(20)], because the teachings of Socrates and Confucius, Jesus and Buddha did not transform humankind.

This book takes the position of another school of thinkers[4,14,15,16]. Here, the Axial Age is not just a spiritual *event*, but a socio-cultural *process of transformation*. As a result, the experiences of the Greeks, Israelites, Indians and Chinese are individual. Each transformation reflects its society's history, existing culture, and local events at the time. That's why Schmuel Eisenstadt calls them "multiple axialities"[17]. Yet the *process* is similar in all.

In Greece and Israel, India and China, the old social order, grounded in the old survival strategies, would break down so thoroughly that people in them would have to *re-form their societies*. New religious approaches were part of that re-formation, but so were new approaches to politics, economics and technology. No longer limited by traditional ways of thinking and acting, they could experiment "with new ways to view the human world"[18(74)]. The breakthroughs that resulted from this experimentation would be tested and eventually institutionalized. And, so, these societies' breakdowns would result in social breakthroughs[14], including the "religions of the book," bureaucratic empires, and increasingly market-oriented economies.

This axial transformation could only occur where the breakdown was complete enough to free people from their old ways of thinking. For instance, the breakthrough of monotheism helped Israelite – and, later, Christian and Islamic – society to develop new institutions that transformed their social survival strategies. Yet, monotheism appeared in both Persian Zoroastrianism and Egypt's pharaoh Akhenaton long before it did in Israel[4]. Persian and Egyptian societies did not break down fully enough for monotheism to transform them. In Greece and Israel, India and China, however, that breakdown was full enough to free people to bring about a thoroughgoing social transformation.

It's worth emphasizing that this sort of axial transformation was in no way "inevitable." It was a specific set of adaptations that occurred in only four Eurasian societies. Axial transformations occurred only where increases in population, advances in technology and growing wealth overwhelmed the existing social network and, then, something new evolved.

The key question this book will explore, then, is: How does a society reinvent itself? To explain the dynamics of social reinvention, we want to introduce a concept we call "world stories"[19]. Any society's world story provides the storehouse of strategies it can use to thrive as a

On stories

In this book, we use the word "story" in a very specific way. To create a story, the storyteller chooses the most important details of an experience, puts them in order, and gives them a point of view[20]. While people usually think of stories as fictions—a play by Shakespeare, a novel by Dostoyevsky, a film by Hitchcock, or what you tell your spouse when he/she "can't handle the truth"—more and more research over the last 25 years suggests that telling stories, to ourselves as well as others, is essential to being human.

In neurobiology, for example, researchers discovered a part of the brain that turns a person's experience into stories. Without that person being conscious of the process, this "interpreter module"[21] weaves together sense impressions and memories into a coherent story so that she can figure out what's happening. In fact, coherence is so important that the brain will "confabulate"—make up details—to fill in things that she doesn't know. Once the brain creates the story, she can decide how to respond to the situation.

Storytelling, then, is the way human beings explain events around them so that they can act on and learn from them. In this way, every person forms a story about the world that is reflected in his or her personality. Every family, organization, religion, profession and state develops a story about how people within it should act toward others in and outside the group.

Research in cultural anthropology further suggests that storytelling began with our evolutionary ancestor, *Homo Erectus*, about 1.8 million years ago[22]. While this early storytellers used mime, gesture and dance, rather than language, their stories enabled them to, communicate and teach each other. In fact, their storytelling helped them spread from Africa to Ice Age Europe, tropical India, and even Australia. By 50,000 years ago, our *Homo Sapiens* ancestors had developed the ability to tell stories with language. With it, they spread across the globe and came to dominate environments from the Arctic Circle to the Amazonian jungles.

Merlin Donald[22] even speculates that storytelling had become such a powerful survival strategy that language evolved in order to tell better stories. Stories in language made it possible for our hunter-gatherer ancestors to remember large amounts of information, including events beyond their lifetimes. It enabled them to draw each other detailed verbal pictures about the movement of animals they hunted or hostile bands. It gave them a way to teach tool making and discuss innovation. It enabled them to create meaning and build order in a chaotic world. It made it possible for them to recreate their social worlds so that they could survive as hunter-gatherers, farmers, city dwellers, and world travelers.

In the end, telling stories with symbolic language may well have been one of the most important advantages human beings had in outlasting their Neanderthal cousins, whose less sophisticated language limited their ability to communicate[18].

However, because storytelling is such a powerful survival strategy, people often come to believe that their stories are the reality they created those stories to explain. If the world changes, people often experience only what was included in their old stories and fail to behave appropriately. So, 17th century Chinese quite accurately thought their seafaring Western visitors were barbarians. What this story hid was that by the 19th century, those barbarians would become capable of inflicting the "hundred years of humiliation" on China. Unless people realize that they experience stories that explain the world, rather than the world itself, those stories can end up being as self-destructive as they once were essential for survival.

culture. Egyptian or Greek mythology, the Torah in Israel or the Vedic literature in India, are all examples of world stories.

Perhaps the most powerful single such story is a society's world story. That power lies in the way they answer some of the most fundamental questions of human life, including:

- What is the origin of human beings, and what do they owe the invisible forces that created and maintain them?

- What does it mean to be members of the group in which one forms an identity, and how should members treat other members and outsiders?
- How should people manage the communities in which they live?
- And perhaps most crucial, in a world where fear and pain are unavoidable, why should anyone choose to live, rather than die?

In answering these questions, world stories present the model for how people in a culture survive and thrive. This model both limits what people who accept any such story can do and think *and* offers a platform for experimentation. World stories do *not*, however, *determine* what people will do. Rather, they act as storehouses of possibilities that people can put in action. With this shared set of stories about how to live in their societies, people can create a social framework for discussing what is happening around them and how to respond. They can then take action on events, and see how effectively their world stories let them deal with the events. If their actions are not successful, people can amend their stories. In this way, world stories provide the model for cultural learning.

Historians have often treated world stories as "religious" or "philosophical." This book treats them differently. For us, the issues labeled "spiritual," "economic," "political," and "technological," are thoroughly interlaced.

While each axial experience was unique, all four followed a common pattern in which their world stories evolve.

That pattern includes six phases, which occurred more or less consecutively:

1. Political fragmentation;
2. Social experiments grounded in foundational stories – a vision of cultural success based on its society's old world story[23];
3. Intensification of warfare;
4. Appearance of a new world story;
5. Developing commentary of that story, so that the society can amend its approach to unexpected challenges, and;
6. Emergence of empire.

In a short book like this, we can only follow this pattern in two cases. We chose the Greek and Chinese axial experiences for two reasons. First, as Alan Watts notes, they are the most different of the "high cultures."[24] If the Greek and Chinese axial experiences follow a similar path, that path should offer a valid model of axial transformation. Second, historians know the most about the Greek and Chinese experiences. (Readers interested in learning more may want to look at [15,23] for the Israelite experience, and [11,15] for the Indian experience.)

Initial conditions

It should not be surprising that Greek and Chinese cultures are so different. After all, people in them had to adapt to very different geographic, social, and economic conditions.

Greece is a land of islands and a small mainland of mountain chains that act as natural barriers. As a result, human communities, even cities, tended to develop as relatively small and politically independent. Moreover, the land was not nearly as rich as that in Mesopotamia, Egypt, or China. Agriculture was largely limited to grapes (wine) and olives (oil), with barley as the only viable grain. To support larger populations, the Greeks had to focus on commerce, and its cities became a nexus for trade between Europe, the Middle East, and Egypt. Greece also became a crossroad for invasions and migrations, including those of the Indo-Europeans, c. 2000 BCE, and of the Sea People, c. 1200 BCE. The combination of their history of invasions and the constant change of an economy based on trade made the creation of order extremely important. Socially, the transformation of chaos to order was ritualized in the *agon*, the formal contest, which appears in events from the Olympics to Plato's dialogues[13].

Chinese culture, on the other hand, emerged in a geographically isolated society of farmers[25,26]. Theirs was a world of familiar faces and routines, tied to the soil and the rituals with which they strove to maintain order. In this world, kinship was the key to survival not merely in their daily life, but in the ancestor worship by which "ancestral spirits" helped maintain "the ritual order"[27(24)]. As a result, "the unit of [social] isolation [was] not the individual, but the group," and the village was the basic social unit[25(40-41)]. Most people lived their lives in one village; so harmony, through submission to authority, was central. In addition, social order depended on people managing their personal networks, as it appears to have been in tribal societies[28]. Law would only become an issue when people were unable to manage those networks[29]. Where the Greeks adopted the *agon* as the ritual for creating order, the Chinese preferred harmony and submission to authority, in rituals of ancestor worship, family life, and kingship.

Yet, in spite of these differences between Greek and Chinese cultures, the dynamics of their axial experiences are remarkably similar. Let us now look at the six phases of their experiences, first the Greek version, then the Chinese.

Fragmentation

The Greek political centers, especially Mycenae, flourished in the 14th and early 13th centuries BCE, prospering from their trade with powers such as Egypt and Ugarit, in today's Syria. However, by 1200 BCE, a series of factors, from over-population to a breakdown in trade, overwhelmed the Greek social system. The "essentially artificial way of life [of the Mycenaeans] ... was unable to take the strain"[6(197)]. Following this breakdown, a dark age spread through much of the Eastern Mediterranean.

In China, the Zhou Dynasty overthrew the Shang c. 1040 BCE. The Zhou expanded their empire, as a succession of kings sent about 200 members of their lineage line to rule domains in their name[30]. Much of that time was peaceful, as Chinese armies stopped fighting Chinese armies. However, as trade and wealth increased, and the loyalty of those lords decreased through much of the 9th century BCE, the power of the central government drained into local power centers[31].

In both cases, the result was political fragmentation. By about 700 BCE, Greece included several hundred *poleis*, city-governed political units; several hundred others resulted from colonizing Asia Minor and the Mediterranean through the 6th century BCE[32]. During the Spring-and-Autumn Period (722-481 BCE) China consisted of as many as 170 small kingdoms[33].

In both, the pre-axial society, whose order depended on aristocrats' loyalty to the king's lineage, could no longer manage their increasing complexity. That complexity can be measured in several ways:

- While there are no population estimates for Greece during the dark ages, its estimated population grew from about 800,000 c. 800 BCE to about 10 million c. 400 BCE[34]. In China, estimated population grew from about 13.5 million in 2200 BCE to about 30-40 million in 221 BCE[35];

- Wealth increased, as cultural centers in Mesopotamia and Egypt, India and China, discovered each other, starting about 1500 BCE. This trade led to an inter-state commerce, especially in the Eastern Mediterranean; it increased desire for prestige possessions among an expanding elite; and it created the need for more craftspeople and merchants, and;

- Technological innovations in writing and manufacture, metallurgy and warfare, enhanced societies' ability to support larger populations. As a result, war became more destructive, and the ability to spread and innovate with new ideas accelerated.

These developments formed a self-reinforcing cycle that would further increase social complexity through the Axial Age .

The concept of social complexity is central to this book. Traditionally, social historians and anthropologists considered it a matter of structure. The more levels of socio-political integration a culture has, the more complex it is[36,37]. More recent work[38,39] views social complexity as a dynamic of cultural evolution. This book focuses mostly on a dynamic understanding. Social complexity increases in response to: increasing population and role diversity in it, advances in knowledge and technology, growth in trade and wealth, and the difficulty of governing larger populations. Because these forces tend to drive each other, social complexity generally increases. That increase has been historically likely but not necessary, occurring in the interplay of factors that drive both stability and change[40]. For example, a high level of social complexity in Europe during the Roman Empire was followed by a lower level in the Medieval period.

Two technologies proved especially important. First, Indo-European herders in the Caucasus began experimenting with iron as early as 2500 BCE, introducing it into the Middle East through trade[3]. Iron was more plentiful and eventually became cheaper than bronze. So, it would be possible to produce highly effective tools that were affordable for larger groups of people. In addition, the Chinese could feed armies of several hundred thousand soldiers in the Axial Age because iron plows increased agricultural productivity. In combination with spoked-wheel chariots and curved compound bows (c. 1000 BCE), iron metallurgy made it possible to transform war from a ritualized battle for honor among aristocrats to a massive exercise in political domination[31].

The other key technology was writing. Writing systems that could effectively communicate spoken language[41(12)] emerged in Mesopotamia and, a little later, Egypt, toward the end of the 4th century BCE, about the time the first states arose. By the middle of the 2nd century BCE, writing had spread throughout the Eastern Mediterranean. The origins of Chinese writing are more mysterious, but the system seems to have developed fully by the middle of the 2nd century BCE[42]. Before the Axial Age, writing remained almost entirely "sectorial"[14(383)] – that is, it was used among a small minority of educated elites, in specific sectors of society. In this way, writing was mostly used for social control, whether among the priests who managed agricultural surpluses or the scribes who served the bureaucracy.

During the Axial Age, however, writing would become the way to communicate culture, from ancient classics to the most recent ideas. With the text in front of them, people could now examine their thought and that of others. This move toward self-reflection is one of the most important innovations of the Axial Age[8]. Writing would also make it possible to accumulate and study much greater bodies of knowledge.

The political fragmentation in Greece and China accelerated the advances in both technology and social innovation. As the many political entities fought for leadership, people in them could try out a wide variety of new ideas, spurred by their competition. What provided the unity that held them together was the foundational stories they held in common.

Foundational stories

Foundational stories articulate group identity as "remembered past," mixing myth and history[23(59)]. This vision of the past created both a template for action and cultural unity in the midst of their political fragmentation. The threat of chaos dominates these stories in both Greece and China.

In Greece that fear appears in Hesiod's stories of Uranus eating his children or Homer's account of how Troy was destroyed as the result of a beauty contest. As painful and frightening as chaos may be, it is part of the natural world from which order emerges, a common element of pre-axial world stories[43]. As in Hesiod's story of the rape of Persephone, an act of violence becomes the basis for the Greek myth of agriculture, the ultimate image of order. Faced with this chaotic and capricious world, Homer weaves a myth of the aristocracies of the small Greek polities as fractious brothers, coming together to protect each other's honor. So they go to war over Helen and defeat the eastern enemy, Troy. Even though the Trojan War appears to be mythic, its style of war is that of the pre-axial states, bronze-age aristocrats fighting for honor.

These Greek foundational stories reflected the simpler, pre-axial world, but also offered models for axial experiments. For instance, the Greek *poleis* resembled the small, independent polities of Homer's epics, united by a common, Hellenistic culture. Yet, the *poleis* were also axial experiments, with their rejection of the traditional concept of kingship, an attempt at government that substitutes a more formal, participatory decision-making process for that of pre-axial family lineages. These experiments offered many approaches – from the militarist oligarchy of Sparta to the commercially democratic Athenians[32].

Much of Greece's Axial Age history seems to act out its foundational stories. Until the Persian Wars at the beginning of the 5th century BCE, the *poleis* behaved like the fractious pre-axial polities Homer depicted in the *Iliad*, going to war periodically. Faced with a common enemy from the East, like Troy, they united to defeat the much larger armies of the Persians in 490 and 480 BCE. Having achieved this success, the *poleis* acted like brothers again, fighting over political and economic control. Without a unifying eastern enemy, their myth of fractious brothers would lead them into the Peloponnesian Wars. It would be in response to the devastation of these wars that Greece's new world story would appear.

The foundational stories that produced a sense of unity among the Chinese kingdoms looked back to a Zhou golden age of peace and prosperity, depicted in one of China's foundational texts, the *Shujing* (*Book of Documents*). By the time of the Zhou, the High God of the earlier Shang Dynasty (*Di*) had been translated into the more abstract concept of Heaven, much like Plato's Realm of Forms, but more imminent within the world of matter. Schwartz calls it an "anthropocosmology in which entities, processes and classes of phenomena found in nature correspond to or 'go together with' various entities, processes, and classes of phenomena in the human world."[27(351)]

This cosmology is very much that of a farmer[26], constantly attending to the cycles and transformations of nature. In this way, Heaven gives birth to Earth[44], and the *Yijing*, the *Book of Changes*, a foundational text that seems to have been formalized c. 1000 BCE, is a guide to the continually transforming world. Order was Heaven's gift, and as long as humans followed the *Dao*, Way of Heaven, order would be the natural result. With divinity dwelling in the world, the mythic actors in China's foundational stories are not gods, but early "sages." For example, Yu created order by inventing irrigation and water control after the Great Flood of the Yellow River, and the kings Yao and Shu set the example for ordered public rule[27,31].

Politically, this worldview appears as the "Mandate of Heaven." When the Zhou overthrew the Shang Dynasty (c. 1040 BCE), the cultural emphasis on submission to authority demanded a justification. So the Duke of Zhou declared that the Shang had lost the "Mandate of Heaven" because of their wickedness and failure to fulfill their ritual duties. In this way, the foundational stories put responsibility on the king, who, through his proper ritual performance could influence his ancestors to intercede with Heaven to maintain order. For more than two millennia, these ideas were the backbone of Chinese political life.

As with the Greek experience, Chinese foundational stories also provided the basis for axial experimentation. The approaches to kingship of the Chinese kingdoms were variations on the theme of returning the order – and unity – that had been lost after the Zhou golden age. This movement toward unity was gradual. The "Spring-and-Autumn" period (771-476 BCE) witnessed a constant state of war; one account lists 540 interstate wars and more than 230 civil wars in a single 259-year period[31(36)]. In pre-axial China, warfare had been, as it was in Greece, an aristocratic exercise in honor. With the fragmentation of power centers, however, war became a destructive exercise in political domination.

By the 6th century BCE, iron was being increasingly used in China, at which time the iron plow appears[45]. As a result, agricultural productivity shot up, as did wealth, population, and the ability of the remaining Chinese kingdoms to field massive armies. By the end of the 6th century BCE, warfare and the terror it spread was everywhere; corruption was rampant; and China's rulers had unquestionably lost the Way of Heaven[27]. By the end of the Spring-and-Autumn period, this warfare had reduced the number of competing states from 170 to seven. The devastation that accompanied it created a nightmare of chaos and drove both a deep sense that something was wrong and the search for how to address it.

To meet the challenge of governing amid such warfare, the great Chinese political experiment would be in bureaucracy. China's traditional ancestor worship contributed little to a bureaucratic way of thinking[46]. As a result, Chinese bureaucracy did not emerge until other religious cults and practices, such as rituals associated with the Mandate of Heaven, overshadowed ancestor worship in official ideology during the Warring States era[47]. So, while Schwartz describes the Shang Dynasty, preceding the Zhou, as "protobureaucratic,"[27(34)] full bureaucracy would emerge only in the Axial Age, with experiments that would culminate in Legalist theories, as we'll see. The ancestor cult continued to be important at the family and community levels of Chinese life into the 20th century; however, at the level of the state, the growing bureaucratization of the state would separate people from those in power[48].

Intensification of war

In axial Greece, the Persian invasions of 490 and 480 BCE and then the Peloponnesian Wars (431-404 BCE) reinforced the fear of chaos expressed in the foundational stories. The invasion of the Persians, vastly wealthier and with far larger armies, must have spread terror throughout the *poleis*, especially when Athens was burnt in 480 BCE. With the Peloponnesian Wars, the need for a new way of governing human life became unmistakable.

At the beginning of that war, the Athenians chose to draw their outlying population behind the city walls. But in 430 BCE, a plague broke out, leading to widespread terror. In addition, rather than fighting to a resolution, the armies of Athens and Sparta pillaged each other's territory[13]. The Greek historian Thucydides described the resulting lawlessness: "No fear of god or law of man had a restraining influence. As for the gods, it seemed to be the same thing whether one worshiped them or not, when one saw the good and the bad dying indiscriminately. As for offenses against human law, no one expected to live long enough to be brought to justice"[15(381)]. The resulting horror reflected not only people's suffering, but also their inability to derive comfort, or even satisfying explanation from their foundational world story.

Dissatisfaction with the old world story is at the heart of the tragedies of Aeschylus, Sophocles, and Euripides, which appeared between the beginning of the Persian Wars in 490 BCE and the end of the Peloponnesian Wars in 404 BCE. These tragedies reflected on how even good people, such as Orestes or Oedipus, become caught in uncontrollable forces, no matter how hard they resist. In this way Greek tragedy could reflect "the political and cultural rise of Athens, its inner corruption, and its disastrous fall . . ."[15(352-3)], during a century of prosperity and war, empire and chaos.

These texts also reflect Timothy Reiss' understanding of tragedy, "appearing at certain moments of seemingly abrupt epistemic change . . . making a new class of discourse possible." Tragedy, then, defines the "moment of rupture," as people recognize that the old ways do not work and new ways of thinking are needed[49(2,21)]. This "tragic" process "*creates order* [from chaos] *and makes it possible to ascribe meaning to that order*" (author's italics)[49(17)]. It would be the new world story, especially as articulated by Plato and Aristotle, that would address the need for the new way of thinking about the world that Greek tragedy announced.

A similar intensification of war dominated China's Warring States period (403-221 BCE). What characterized the seven remaining kingdoms was "the unquestioned supremacy of a single, cosmically potent autocrat who ruled as the image of Heaven on earth, and the reconstitution of the public order around this figure through new forms of interpersonal ties and the extension of military service to the entire population of the state"[31(246)]. Warfare became the extension of the will of a single commander. Such commanders were supported by a growing literature of military science, for which Suntzi's *Art of War* was only the best-known example. Over this period, advances in technology, such as the crossbow, continued to intensify warfare[31]. By 300 BCE, even Mencius (c. 372-289 BCE), the Chinese thinker most convinced of the goodness of people, recognized that only the unity provided by a single king could restore social order[27].

The Chinese axial period did not produce an explicit tragic literature, as in Greece. Still, a similar tragic awareness of the need for a different way of running society emerged in the flowering of philosophic thought with the "*shih*," wandering scholars. These cast-off surplus sons of the office-holding aristocracy, such as Confucius[27,44], both preached their thought and sought positions counseling kings.

Like the Greeks, they used written texts to reflect on the loss of order. However, the Chinese believed that order was Heaven's gift, a belief the Zhou Dynasty had realized.

So they focused on why people introduce disorder by deviating from the Way they know will create a good society. From the 5th through the 3rd centuries BCE, the *shih* would form the "hundred schools" of philosophy[26]. These "schools" reflected various currents of thought, responding to the chaos of their time, and many of them contain elements of the tragic insight, the desire for a lost order that would make the new world story necessary.

New world stories

In Greece, the new world story was a dream of rational order. It would be negotiated over several hundred years, in several schools of natural philosophy, beginning with the Milesian "physicists" such as Thales (c. 625-547 BCE). These thinkers examined the natural world from a variety of positions. For example:

- Heraclitus (fl. c. 500 BCE) believed the world was in constant flux;

- The Atomists, such as Democritus (c. 470-404 BCE), saw a world of atoms obeying invariable laws of nature, "a lifeless piece of machinery"[50(29-30)], and;

- Pythagoras (c. 580-500 BCE) conceived of a cosmos ruled by the harmony of numbers.

Other thinkers focused on society. The Sophists, for instance, examined politics and the rhetoric essential to it. One of their most noted thinkers, Protagoras (c. 490-420 BCE), taught his students to question everything, including the gods, and argued that, not those gods, but man should be "the measure of all things." All this thought, rejected, accepted, or modified, would be canonized in the world story largely established in the philosophy of Plato (c. 428-347 BCE) and the practical applications of Aristotle (384-322 BCE).

Plato grew up near Athens during the Peloponnesian Wars, and as a man of about 30 watched the citizens of Athens execute his teacher, Socrates. In many ways, Plato's writings became an attempt to answer the Axial Age version of the world story questions: What is the origin and purpose of human life? How can we be so terrifyingly destructive to each other? And how could the *polis* best govern itself in order to contain the chaos that such destruction causes?

Plato's answer was that the design of the universe was orderly and rational, even though the universe itself might be messy and chaotic. However, understanding that design would enable some people to govern effectively. Rejecting the pre-axial gods, Plato argued for a creative spirit, the Demiurge (*Timaeus*), who was benevolent and desired to create order in the world, based on the abstract Forms of things. The true reality of any thing is in the rational, abstract Form from which the Demiurge created it, not the messy, chaotic examples one sees in everyday life.

Thus, in *Republic* (c. 380 BCE), he writes, "Until the person is able to abstract and define rationally the idea of good ... he knows neither the idea of good nor any other good; he apprehends only a shadow..." This attempt to define the universe as essentially rational is reflected in Plato's emphasis on mathematics as a prerequisite for philosophical study, as well as his enthusiasm for understanding the movement of the planets through mathematics[51]. Change, in Plato's world story, is an illusion. It is in their identities, derived from divine Forms, that things are real[52].

In this world, where abstract Forms are more real than what humans experience, chaos did not enter as a result of the Demiurge's design, but because of the material with which the Demiurge worked[15]. As Plato details in his Parable of the Cave (*Republic*), most people live in a world of "shadows," dominated by emotion and appetite, content with the old mythos, the unfalsifiable stories of mythology. They are unable to perceive the Forms. To avoid the chaos that Athens had experienced during the Peloponnesian Wars, Plato offered an "alternative basis for Greek culture" [53(414)], replacing Homer's heroic ideal with that of the *theoros*, the philosopher who "loves the spectacle of truth"[54(98)]. The *theoros* would allow most citizens to have their *mythos*, but they themselves would live by the rational, "falsifiable" *logos* – the stories of logical examination.

Aristotle, born after the Peloponnesian Wars, "was able calmly to look around the new world that Plato had opened up and explore its many possibilities, without rancor"[15(395-6)]. Plato's Demiurge would become Aristotle's "Unmoved Mover," a divinity of pure thought, beyond our world of matter, and the cosmos it created. Below the Moon was our chaotic, ever changing world; above it, the unchanging Heavens[50(28)], rotating in perfect crystalline spheres. Humans created chaos only because they would not allow the pure intellect of the divine to guide them. Chaos was no longer a part of the natural world, as it had been in pre-axial times, but a perversion of it. To avoid chaos, the *polis* must train citizens in using their reason.

Aristotle's many other studies continued to apply his own rational principle to one field of study after another, answering the questions behind any world story. His *Ethics*, for example, explored how the individual could achieve *eudaimonia* – "happiness" or "welfare" – to live the life of *theoria*. Similarly, in his *History of Animals*, Aristotle explained the place of human beings in the created world by embellishing the Great Chain of Being that Plato had hinted at with his ideas about divine plenitude in *Timaeus*, to indicate that man was greater than the beasts but lesser than the angels[55]. In these and other explorations, Aristotle would "sketch out most of the fields of inquiry that would preoccupy later thinkers"[15(395)].

One final thinker would complete the Greek world story. Epicurus (341-270 BCE) was born long after both the glories and terrors of the 5th century BCE. Like Plato and Aristotle, he assumed that the world is rationally knowable. As a result, he insisted that nothing should be believed, except that which was tested through direct observation and logical deduction. Contrary to Plato and Aristotle, he was sure that senses, not reason, can help establish truth and lead people to realize what is good and therefore desirable, as well as what is not. For that reason, the task of each person is to maximize happiness and minimize harm to themselves and others. Such a life should be lived without drawing attention to oneself. Living in the Athenian *polis* in decline, Epicurus, advocated seclusion from political activities. This pulling away from the political life that had been so important in the 5th century BCE, reflected Epicurus' belief that the gods, unlike those of Homer, had no interest in human beings. Instead, they enjoyed constant bliss in the space between infinite spontaneously developing worlds. For Epicurus, society arose as a contract between people, with the aim of causing no harm to each other. However, they tended to forget that they can change all the laws and customs to serve their mutual benefit[55,57,58].

While this dream of order in the Greek new world story was rational, in China, it was social. Han Dynasty historian Sima Qian (d. 86 BCE) divided the many varieties of Chinese philosophy into six meta-schools[27,44]. Each of these schools drew deeply on traditional thought, as one might expect in a culture of ancestor worship. Three are critical for understanding the new Chinese world story – Confucianism, Daoism, and Legalism.

For Confucians, the ideal social order had already existed in the Zhou's "universal, all-embracing, ethicopolitical order"[27(65)]. In this golden age, the king carefully fulfilled his ritual duties, behaving with *ren*, translated "benevolence" or "kindheartedness"[27]. Only by re-establishing that order could chaos be tamed. To do so, Confucius (551-479 BCE) and his followers focused on the need for people to live according to the ritual formulas for their positions. Confucians also emphasized education as a means for both individuals and society at large to understand the *Dao*, the "Way." The Confucian Way focused on society, demanding that:

- People observe *li*, the appropriate ritual behavior, in all actions;

- Relationships exist as a network of dyads – husband/wife, father/son, ruler/minister, for instance – in which the former had both power and the responsibility to take care of the latter, and;
- Those in charge of government know the "proper" way to do all things, as articulated by the ancestors, hence the critical importance of education.

The ideal king would set an example that could be reenacted through the personal networks that flowed from him, throughout government and society, just as village elders had been responsible in China's traditional farming culture. The king's example was central. While law was necessary for extreme cases – the Chinese word for law, *fa*, also means "punishment" – it could not enforce orderly behavior throughout a society so deeply dependent on relationships. As Graham summarizes his thought:

What Confucius dreams of is a society in which civilized behavior will 'just come naturally' ... The tao can, in fact, be restored to the world only by the noble man's sustained conscious efforts, by painstaking self-scrutiny, scrupulous attention to behavior, unflagging devotion to the cultivation of learning, attentive practice of li and conscientious service in government.[44(189)]

Politically, Confucius viewed the state as a family or clan, and the king as a family or a clan head[59,60]. These ideas were rooted deeply in the pre-axial popular religious beliefs[47], especially China's ancestor cult[61(379)].

While Confucius's teachings would dominate post-axial Chinese thought, they had little effect in his lifetime. War and chaos continued to intensify, and several responses emerged. Within Confucianism, the increasingly intense warfare set off a debate on the nature of humankind. Mencius (c. 372-289 BCE) held that human nature was essentially good and that force alone was not sufficient to produce order; the good king must win "the hearts of the people by benevolent government"[44(113)]. Still, the chaos of war convinced Mencius that order demanded a single ruler for China. On the other hand, Xunzi (c. 312-230 BCE) held that human nature was evil. The purpose of government, then, was to curb the desires of inferior people and convince them to accept their places. Xunzi's belief in government-imposed social control would remain central to Confucian thought and be used extensively to achieve order in post-axial China.

For the Daoists, the overly civilized order of the Confucians had made it impossible for people to behave naturally, in harmony with the Way and the Heaven-given laws of change[44]. Only when people learned the *Dao* and acted according to it, would order return. As Bellah notes, in both major Daoist texts, the *Zhuangzi* (attributed to Zhuangzi, c. 369-286 BCE) and the *Daodejing* (attributed to Laozi, alternately identified as a contemporary of Confucius and a government official in the first half of the 4th century BCE),"things started out well when humans were merged with nature, but began to go downhill when culture was invented."[16(447)] Where Confucius thought of the *Dao* as Heaven's plan for the way of man in society, the Daoists seemed to think of it as the flow of the Universe, the "transformation of *qi* [energy]" (Zhang Zai, as quoted in [62(22)]) as the "myriad things" of this world engage in their ongoing process of interacting and affecting each other[52]. From this perspective, events have a rhythm of their own, and the wise person, the "sage," can use an understanding of that rhythm to achieve his or her ends.

The road to a properly ordered society requires a king depending on a sage who understands the *Dao*. Such a sage can help the king structure society so that people will effortlessly behave in a way that produces order. This Daoist position relies on a deep, almost mystical connection with the world, rather than the Confucian attempt to control through highly structured relationships. In fact, the Daoist sage must "forget" all the socially imposed "learning" that blocks the ability to perceive the natural flow of the *Dao*[44]. As a result of this connection to the *Dao*, the sage exhibits *wu-wei*, "effortless action." The sage will therefore behave in ways that both express his or her deepest self and conform to the movement of the Way, where "proper conduct follows as instantly and spontaneously as the nose responds to a bad smell"[63(8)].

For the Legalists, the chaos of the Warring States period resulted from the unruliness of human nature. That unruliness could only be tamed with clear, harshly enforced laws[26]. In doing so, two Legalists – Shang Yang (390-338 BCE) and Han Feizi (280-230 BCE) – would be largely responsible for making Qin the Warring States kingdom that would unite China. For Han Feizi, agriculture and warfare were the two legitimate activities in the state, and warfare, "the primary institution used by the rulers of state to organize, rank, and control their subjects"[31](67). To translate this policy into social reality, Legalist advisors to the king of Qin:

- Divided the state into counties and the counties into small groups. People could then be punished for the crimes of others in their groups. This division also made it easier to record population and recruit for the army;

- Promoted soldiers through the military hierarchy based on how many enemies they had killed;

- Abolished the aristocracy and freed farmers to buy and sell land;

- Introduced a comprehensive tax system that exempted farmers and clothing makers who exceeded their production targets, and;

- Instituted harsh, but uniform laws that applied to everyone in the state.

All these reforms were to function automatically, rather than at the will of ruler or bureaucrats.

Legalist bureaucracy functioned "much closer in conception to Weber's modern ideal-type than to a notion of patrimonial bureaucracy"[27](336). It relied on competitive tests to grant positions, rather than personal influence, and rewarded ministers who exceeded their objectives. As a result, Han Feizi helped create a state, driven almost mechanically, "by reliance on the negative and positive incentives of a universal, objective, and impersonal system of penal laws and rewards"[27](332). Han Feizi developed this bureaucracy when he served the king of Qin, who would become the First Emperor, *Qin*

Shi Huang. At some point, however, the king became suspicious of him and had him commit suicide in 230 BCE. In spite of that, Han Feizi's principles formed the bedrock ideology of the Qin Dynasty, implemented by his successor Li Si (c. 280-208 BCE).

As a result of the ardor with which the First Emperor applied that ideology, his memory is both loved and regretted. Not only did he unify a state weary of war and develop a program of road and waterway building. Leagalism's insistence on standards also led him to develop a uniform written language that enabled people with China's many dialects to communicate, as well as uniform standards for roads, weights, and currency. On the other hand, because he relied on Legalist advice, he is also remembered for burying 460 scholars alive and for the book burning beginning in 213 BCE, as well as for exorbitant taxation. Legalism thus developed a bad reputation and appears to have been ignored in China's commentary period. Still, its principles became deeply woven into the Chinese conception of government, down through the Communism of Mao[29].

Commentary on the world story

Assmann describes the period of commentary as "an indispensable accompaniment to the cultural transformation ... keeping those texts alive by bridging the ever widening gap between them and the changing reality of life"[23(269)]. During the Greek and Chinese commentary periods, Alexander the Great spread Hellenism; Rome rose in the West; and the Qin united

China at the end of the Axial Age. During this period, which continued to develop the new world stories long after the "end" of the Axial Age in 200 BCE, population and wealth increased, and technology accelerated. Commentary on the new world story would enable people to make adjustments to the ways of governing and behaving in their increasingly complex societies.

In Greece, this commentary would play itself out, first of all, in the philosophy of thinkers such as the Cynics, Stoics, Epicureans, and Neo-Platonists in the Hellenistic period. It would also develop in early scientific thinkers, mostly located in Alexandria, including:

- Eratosthenes, who drew the first map of the known world on a grid of latitude and longitude;
- Aristarchus, who used geometry to estimate the size of the Earth by comparing its movements to those of the Sun and Moon, and;
- Ptolemy, whose mapping of the movements of the planets with epicycles was accepted until the Renaissance, along with his speculations on optics, geography and musical theory[51].

Later, as Rome embraced Christianity, Fathers of the Church, such as Augustine and Origen, would further comment on this world story, drawing especially on concepts such as a soul separate from the body, the divinity as an Unmoved Mover, and the emphasis on moral distinctions. Many of these assumptions would be integrated into the world story of the Roman Empire, the Byzantine Empire, and then that of Western culture.

The Chinese commentary period seems to have been underway by the beginning of the 4th century BCE. Throughout it, Chinese thinkers of all schools would borrow from each other extensively. Han Feizi, for example, was a student of the Confucian Xunzi, borrowing his belief that human beings were essentially evil; he also borrowed from Daoist Laozi's ideas about the Way and *wu-wei*, to provide a metaphysical justification for his emphasis on punishment[44]. Throughout the subsequent millennium and a half, this discourse, largely between Confucians, Daoists, and, later, Buddhists, would continue, as different dynasties employed ministers of different beliefs. Finally, a mature form of Neo-Confucianism took form in the 15th century CE.

Empire emerges

In both Greece and China, the Axial Age concluded with empire building, which would lead to the conquests of Alexander, Rome in the early post-axial period, and the Qin and, then, the Han dynasties in China. A similar period of empires would emerge in India. It seems that the great social lesson of these axial experiences was that the more complex societies that had evolved required a single steady hand to wring order from the chaos. This common end point is particularly provocative given the vast differences in the world stories of Greece and China. While the Chinese story, from its foundational roots in the mythology of Zhou culture, suggests the necessity of a single unified society, the Greek story seems much more compatible with significant differences and multiple power centers.

In any case, without a more detailed examination of all four examples of the Axial Age transformation, any conclusions can only be tentative. What seems clear, however, is that the self-reinforcing cycle of increased population, advancing knowledge and technology, and more trade and wealth drove both the Greeks and Chinese to a survival strategy that included bureaucratic empire. And the really provocative question is how much we have to learn about Modernity when we treat it as a second axial age, to which we now turn.

References

1. Lewis, M.E. (1990). Sanctioned Violence in Early China, Albany, NY: State University of New York Press.

2. Modelski, G. (2003). World Cities, -3000 to 2000, Washington, DC: Faros 2000.

3. Anthony, D.W. (2007). The Horse, the Wheel and Language: How Bronze-age Riders from the Eurasian Steppes Shaped the Modern World, Princeton, NJ: Princeton University Press.

4. Assmann, J. (2008). Of God and Gods: Egypt, Israel, and the Rise of Monotheism, Madison, WI: University of Wisconsin Press.

5. Cline, E.H. (2014). 1177 BC: The Year Civilization Collapsed, Princeton, NJ: Princeton University Press.

6. Sandars, N.K. (1978). The Sea Peoples: Warriors of the Ancient Mediterranean 1250-1150 BC, London, UK: Thames and Hudson.

7. Fairbank, J.K. and Goldman, M. (2006). China: A New History, 2nd ed., Cambridge, MA: Belknap Press.

8. Jaspers, K. (1953). The Origins and Goal of History, Bullock, M. (trans.), New Haven, CT and London, UK: Yale University Press.

9. Voegelin, E. (1957). Order and History, Baton Rouge, LA: Louisiana State University Press.

10. Eisenstadt, S.N. (1982). "The Axial Age: The emergence of transcendental vision and the rise of clerics," Archives Européennes de Sociologie, Vol. 23(2): 294-314.

11. Eisenstadt, S.N. (ed.) (1986). The Origins and Diversity of Axial Age Civilizations, Albany, NY: State University of New York Press.

12. Neville, R.C. (2002). Religion in Late Modernity, Albany, NY: State University of New York Press.

13. Armstrong, K. (2006). The Great Transformation: The Beginning of Our Religious Traditions, New York, NY: Knopf.

14. Assmann, J. (2012). "Cultural memory and the myth of the Axial Age," in R.N. Bellah and H. Joas (eds.), The Axial Age and Its Consequences, Cambridge, MA: The Belknap Press, pp. 366-407.

15. Bellah, R.N. (2011). Religion in Human Evolution: From the Paleolithic to the Axial Age, Cambridge, MA: The Belknap Press.

16. Bellah, R.N. (2012). "The heritage of the Axial Age: Resource or burden?" in R.N. Bellah and H. Joas (eds.), The Axial Age and Its Consequences, Cambridge, MA: The Belknap Press, pp. 447-67.

17. Eisenstadt, S.N. (ed.) (2002). Multiple Modernities, New Brunswick, NJ: Transaction Publications.

18. Donald, M. (2012). "An evolutionary approach to culture: Implications for the study of the Axial Age," in R.N. Bellah and H. Joas (eds.), The Axial Age and Its Consequences, Cambridge, MA: The Belknap Press, pp. 47-76.

19. Baskin, K. (2013). "The complexity of evolution: History as a post-Newtonian social science," Social Evolution and History, Vol. 12(1): 3-27.

20. Bal, M. (1997). Narratology: Introduction to the Theory of Narrative, 2nd ed., Toronto, ON: University of Toronto Press.

21. Gazzaniga, M.S. (2011). Who's in Charge? Free Will and the Science of the Brain, New York, NY: HarperCollins.

22. Donald, M. (1991). Origins of the Modern Mind: Three Stages in the Evolution of Culture and Cognition, Cambridge, MA: Harvard University Press.

23. Assmann, J. (2011). Cultural Memory and Early Civilization: Writing, Remembrance, and Political Imagination, New York, NY: Cambridge University Press.

24. Watts, A. (1975). Tao: The Watercourse Way, New York, NY: Pantheon Books.

25. Fei, X. (1992). From the Soil: The Foundations of Chinese Society, Hsiang t'u C. (trans.), Berkeley, CA: University of California Press.

26. Feng, Y. (1976). A Short History of Chinese Philosophy: A Systematic Account of Chinese Thought from Its Origins to the Present Day, Bodde, D (ed.), New York, NY: The Free Press.

27. Schwartz, B.I. (1985). The World of Thought in Ancient China, London, UK: The Belknap Press.

28. Diamond, J. (2012). The World until Yesterday: What Can We Learn from Traditional Societies? New York, NY: Viking.

29. Baskin, K. (2007). "Ever the twain shall meet," Chinese Management Studies, Vol. 1(1): 57-68.

30. Ebrey, P.B. (1996). The Cambridge Illustrated History of China, Cambridge, UK: Cambridge University Press.

31. Lewis, M.E. (1990). Sanctioned Violence in Early China, Albany, NY: State University of New York Press.

32. Hansen, M.H. (2006). Polis: An Introduction to the Ancient Greek City-State, Oxford, UK: Oxford University Press.

33. Fairbank, J.K. and Goldman, M. (2006). China: A New History, 2nd ed., Cambridge, MA: Belknap Press.

34. Hansen, M.H. (2006). The Shotgun Method: The Demographics of the Ancient Greek City-State Culture, Columbia, MO: University of Missouri Press.

35. Chang-Qun, D., Xue-Chun, G., Wang, J., and Chien, P.K. (1998). "Relocation of civilization centers in Ancient China: Environmental factors," Ambio, Vol. 27(7): 572-575.

36. Bondarenko, D.M. (2007). "Approaching 'Complexity' in Anthropology and Complexity Studies: The principles of socio-political organization and prospects for bridging the interdisciplinary gap", Emergence: Complexity and Organization, Vol. 9(3): 55-67.

37. Bondarenko, D.M. (2007). "What is there in a word?: Heterarchy, homoarchy, and the difference in understanding 'complexity' in the social sciences and complexity studies," in K.A. Richardson and P. Cilliers (eds.),

Explorations in Complexity Thinking: Pre-Proceedings of the 3rd International Workshop on Complexity and Philosophy, Mansfield, MA: ISCE Publishing, pp. 35-48.

38. Friedman, J. and Rowlands, M.J. (1978). "Notes toward an epigenetic model of the evolution of 'civilization'," in J. Friedman and M.J. Rowlands (eds.), The Evolution of Social Systems, Pittsburgh, PA: University of Pittsburgh Press, pp. 201-276.

39. Spooner, B. (2013). "Investment and translocality: Recontextualizing the Baloch in Islamic and global history," http://crossroads-asia.de/fileadmin/user_upload/news/wp14_Spooner_Brian_Baloch_identities.pdf.

40. Lozny, L.R. (2000). "Social complexity: Necessity or chance?" in D.M. Bondarenko and I.V. Sledzevski (eds.), Hierarchy and Power in the History of Civilizations. Abstracts of International Conference, Moscow: Institute for African Studies Press, pp. 79-80.

41. Fischer, S.R. (2001). A History of Writing, London, UK: Reaktion Books.

42. Pankenier, D.W. (2011). "Getting 'right' with Heaven and the origins of writing in China," in L. Feng and D.P. Branner (eds.), Writing and Literacy in Early China: Studies from the Columbia Early China Seminar, Seattle, WA: University of Washington Press, pp. 19-50.

43. Taylor, C. (2012). "What was the axial revolution?" R.N. Bellah and H. Joas (eds.), The Axial Age and Its Consequences, Cambridge, MA: The Belknap Press, pp. 30-46.

44. Graham, A.C. (1989). Disputers of the Tao: Philosophical Argument in Ancient China, Chicago, IL: Open Court Publishing.

45. Temple, R. (2007). The Genius of China: 3,000 Years of Science, Discovery and Invention, Rochester, VT: Inner Tradition.

46. Bondarenko, D.M. (2008). "Kinship, territoriality and the early state lower limit," Social Evolution and History, Vol. 7(1): 19-53.

47. Baum, R. (2004). "Ritual and rationality: Religious roots of the bureaucratic state in Ancient China," Social Evolution and History, 3(1): 41–68.

48. Hsu, F.L.K. (1948). Under the Ancestors' Shadow: Chinese Culture and Personality, New York, NY: Columbia University Press.

49. Reiss, T.J. (1980). Tragedy and Truth: Studies in the Development of a Renaissance and Neoclassical Discourse, New Haven, CT: Yale University Press.

50. Lindberg, D.C. (2007). The Beginnings of Western Science: The European Scientific Tradition in Philosophical, Religious and Institutional Context, Prehistory to A.D. 1450, 2nd ed., Chicago, IL: University of Chicago Press.

51. Freely, J. (2012). Before Galileo: The Birth of Modern Science in Medieval Europe, New York, NY: Overlook Duckworth.

52. Jullien, F. (2004). A Treatise on Efficacy: Between Western and Chinese Thinking, Lloyd, J. (trans.), Honolulu, HI: University of Hawai'i Press.

53. Sullivan, W.M. (2012). "The axial invention of education and today's global knowledge culture," in R.N. Bellah and H. Joas (eds.), The Axial Age and Its Consequences, Cambridge, MA: The Belknap Press, pp. 411-29.

54. Nightingale, A. (2004). Spectacles of Truth in Classical Greek Philosophy: Theoria in Its Cultural Context, Cambridge, UK: Cambridge University Press.

55. Pyne, L.V. and Pyne, S.J. (2012). The Last Lost World: Ice Ages, Human Origins, and the Invention of the Pleistocene, New York, NY: Viking.

56. De Witt, N.W. (1954). Epicurus and His Philosophy, Minneapolis, MN: University of Minnesota Press.

57. Rist, J.M. (1972). Epicurus: An Introduction, Cambridge, MA: Cambridge University Press.

58. Fish, J. and Sanders, K.R., eds. (2011). Epicurus and the Epicurean Tradition, Cambridge, UK: Cambridge University Press.

59. Hsü, L.S. (2005). The Political Philosophy of Confucianism: An Interpretation of the Social and Political Ideas of Confucius, His Forerunners, and His Early Disciples, Abingdon, VA: Routledge.

60. Bell, D.A. (ed.) (2008). Confucian Political Ethics, Princeton, NJ: Princeton University Press.

61. Stepugina, T. V. (2004). "Gosudarstvo i obshchestvo v drevnem Kitae" ["The state and society in Ancient China"], in E.A. Grantovskij and T.V. Stepugina (eds.), Gosudarstvo na Drevnem Vostoke [The State in the Ancient East], Moscow, RU: Vostochnaja Literatura, pp. 375-448.

62. Zhang, D. (2002). Key Concepts in Chinese Philosophy, New Haven, CT: Yale University Press.

63. Slingerland, E. (2003). Effortless Action: Wu-Wei as Conceptual Metaphor and Spiritual Ideal in Early China, Oxford, UK: Oxford University Press.

Chapter 2

Modernity as a second Axial Age

The dream of rational order

Introduction

The mind's deepest desire, even in its most elaborate operations, parallels man's unconscious feeling in the face of his universe...

— Albert Camus, *The Myth of Sisyphus*

Walk through the Gallery of the Academy in Florence, and you can almost see an old world story dying as a new one emerges. Paintings through the 14th and much of the 15th centuries CE still tell the medieval Christian world story – religious subjects, allegorical groupings, and stylized portraits, with gold backgrounds to distance their religious subjects from the viewer.

Then, every once in a while, something alien looks out, as if it were hiding behind the medieval style[1]. For example, in Giottino's "Madonna and Child" (c. 1366), the scene is traditional, except for the portrait of John the Baptist in the lower left corner. While John appears in the same position in many similar portraits, his face here seems out of place – not at all religious, looking, almost mockingly, at the viewer[2(91)]. By the end of the 15th century, the story has shifted further. By Filippino Lippi's

1496 portraits of John the Baptist and Mary Magdalene, the artist portrays the feelings of individuals[2(42)].

With Michelangelo's "David," finished in 1504, the emerging world story stands complete: An individual human being as heroic as any figure from Homer awaits the moment of his personal test. Here, then, is the world story associated with the "modern" era, focused on the human and innovative, in contrast to the medieval focus on the divine and traditional.

But what is Modernity? Is it a radical break from the medieval Christian world, as Karl Marx's Communism or Max Weber's early 20th century sociology propose, or an extended exploration of medieval Christianity's deepest conflicts[3]? A unique reflection of Western Capitalism[4] or a different way to express the same drives and impulses that had existed for more than 5000 years[5]? Does Modernity demonstrate a "European miracle" that would let Westerners dominate the world[6] or merely a Western sweep of history's grand pendulum[7] before returning East?

In this chapter, we want to examine Modernity, starting about 1500 CE, as a period of cultural transformation, a second axial age. Why do we choose that date? For one thing, it's convenient, a nice, round number, but it's also arbitrary. Still, within twenty years of this date, many key events occurred – from Michelangelo's "David" (1504) to Columbus's "discovery" of America (1492) or Vasco de Gama's sailing to India (1498), from Luther's Ninety-five Theses (1517) to Copernicus's early draft of his heliocentric theory (before 1514).

Besides, if Modernity is a second axial age, then we should see evidence of increasing social complexity beginning to threaten the older social survival strategy. For example:

- World population had certainly increased since the end of the Axial Age. From the beginning of the Common Era to 1600 CE, it more than doubled, from about 250 million to nearly 600 million[8(31)];
- The amount of wealth and intensity of trade also accelerated. Starting with the Islamic conquests of the 7th and 8th centuries CE, societies in Eurasia became increasingly connected until, by the Mongol conquests in the 13th century, "many parts of the Old World began to become integrated into a system of exchange from which all apparently benefited"[9(3)];
- Finally, a series of technological innovations – printing, commercially efficient machines, and guns, as well as advances in physics, optics, and astronomy[10] – combined to accelerate social change, demanding new survival strategies.

While the Axial Age and Modernity both responded to increased social complexity, they also differ in important ways. The Axial Age transformations could occur independently in four geographically separated societies that would begin to interact more and more during the period. The social survival strategies created in those societies gave states, especially in the Ottoman and Chinese Empires, an almost unshakable order. So it would fall to Western Europe, which had experienced 1000 years of repeated social breakdowns

– to begin reintegrating a millennium and a half of social experiments. And the world story that would evolve in Europe would then spill across a globe whose societies were in the process of forging a global community.

The modern process of social transformation follows a pattern of social evolution much like that of axial Greece and China, occurring in a series of phases:

1. Political fragmentation;
2. Emergence of foundational stories and social experiments based on them;
3. Intensification of warfare;
4. Appearance of a new world story
5. Developing commentary of that story, and;
6. Emergence of Empire.

Political fragmentation

As with the Axial Age transformations, Western Europe in 1500 CE was both politically fragmented and culturally unified[11,12]. Throughout the late Middle Ages, nation-states-to-be were beginning to emerge, for instance, in England, Spain, France, and Holland; Italy was a collection of city-states; and Germany, of principalities.

Yet they had all experienced a millennium of common forces and events. First, the memory of the Roman Empire and the spread of Christianity had created a common cultural background. Next, they were subject to a millennium of invasions – from the Franks and

Vandals in the 5th century to Islam's conquest of Spain in the 8th century and its continued threat through the 16th, from more than 200 years of Viking raids beginning at the end of the 8th century to the Mongol conquests into Eastern Europe in the 13th century. Throughout, new influences continued to stir the cultural mix, especially through trade and the introduction of new technologies. For example, peaceful interaction with Muslims enriched European thought. That contact reinforced Greek rationalism, making translations available, first from the Neo-Platonist tradition and then the works of Aristotle. Muslim contact also increased trade and introduced developments from India and China. And, of course, the Catholic Church remained an institutional constant. Still, its conflicts with various governments, as they fought to see whether church or state would dominate, would create additional instability, especially in the half millennium leading to 1500 CE[3,13].

These many influences would start coming together in a foundational story that had already begun to emerge at the end of the 12th century CE.

Foundational story

Modernity's foundational story faced a tricky challenge. It would have to integrate the very different worldviews of the Christian spiritual tradition and the restless spirit of the Germanic tribes that invaded Western Europe in the 5th and 6th centuries. To do so, it put together two important stories at the end of the 12th century, when European Medievalism – economic, social, and cultural –

was at its fullest. First, the Arthurian Grail Quest literature, beginning with Chretien de Troyes's *Percival*, combined these worldviews in the quest knights, searching for the object with which they would save their own souls and their culture[14].

Most readers know about the grail quest, if only from movies such as *Excalibur* or *Indiana Jones and the Last Crusade*. The story has even become part of the language, as when someone describes the search for the Higgs boson as "the quest for the holy grail of physics." Still, it's worth recounting the basics of the story: After uniting England, Arthur commits a great sin. As a result, his kingdom is plunged into poverty and misery. The only way to heal the kingdom is for his knights to find the holy grail from which Jesus drank at the last supper. That cup had been brought to England earlier, but lost. The knights search for years, experiencing all sorts of trials and humiliations. Finally, one finds it, and, when Arthur drinks from it, the kingdom is saved.

This salvation was also the theme of a second story – millenarianism, the expectation that the end of days described in the *Book of Revelations* was near. Starting around 1000 CE, expectation of the coming Apocalypse grew. In 1065, several thousand Germans went to Jerusalem to witness Jesus' return. The First Crusade (1096-99) was also widely experienced as part of this story, a "war fought on behalf of God and in fulfillment of His plan"[15](xiii). As Joachim of Fiore (c. 1132-1202) described this apocalyptic vision, the world was approaching a new age. Armageddon, the ultimate battle between good and evil, would be followed by Christ's second coming, the ascend of the elite to

Heaven, a new paradisaical age in which God would be King of the Earth, and "the restoration of mankind to its original God-likeness,"[16(10)]. The vanguard to the new age were the *viri spirituales*, spiritual men, "the order of monks to whom the last great times are given" (Joachim, as quoted in [16(25)]). This sense that the work of mankind was to aid the coming of this age of salvation was translated in the Grail Quest stories to the individual quest knights, who are to redeem their souls and society from chaos, misery, and devastation.

At the end of the 12th century, the grail quest literature championed the authority of a social order joining the Catholic Church and the feudal economic/political class. Yet, events continued to provoke chaos. The loss of Jerusalem in 1187 was followed by the failure of the Third Crusade (1189-92) to retake it. As a result, many people questioned the legitimacy of the Papacy's claim to represent God on Earth. The power of the Church was further reduced in repeated conflicts between the Pope and the secular rulers[13]. The Mongol invasions of the 13th century both threatened Western Europe and created a "world economy" that preceded Wallerstein's 16th century "world-system"[9]. Increasing trade and wealth built the fortunes that would finance the Renaissance, but would also encourage corruption in the Church, especially the Papal indulgences, which would outrage John Wycliffe (c. 1328-1384), Jan Hus (C. 1369-1415) and Martin Luther (1483-1546). Finally, the combination of the Black Plague (1348-50) and the Hundred Years War between England and France (1327-1453) devastated Europe's population crushing any incipient sense of social order[3].

Given the limited purpose of this book, it is impossible to treat the wide variety of social experiments that emerged in the High Middle Ages and would be expressed in Modernity. Those experiments include the acceleration of scientific discoveries and theory[10,17], an "industrial revolution" driven my widespread use of machines[18], and an explosion of commercial experimentation[9,19]. As a result, this period was extremely rich in the innovations of metaphorical quest knights, who included theologian Thomas Aquinas (1225-74), proto-scientist Roger Bacon (c. 1220-1292) and Medici family founder, Giovanni di Bicci de' Medici (c. 1360-1429). However, two such innovations caused ripples of transformational change across the period and thus demand attention here.

As in the Axial Age, advances in communications and manufacturing were transforming the culture. In communications, Gutenberg's printing press with movable type in the mid-15th century brought together a wide variety of social experiments – from advances in metallurgy to European paper manufacture and growing demand for books. As Elizabeth Eisenstein notes [20], the printing press did not merely make inexpensive books widely available. It also:

- Made political and religious propaganda cheap;
- Enabled wide distribution of books in the vernacular, driving the Reformation and early national cultures, and;
- Spread the knowledge and innovation that made the "Scientific Revolution" of the 17th century possible.

Finally, the ability to publish and read the thoughts of many others helped create Modernity's tendency toward intensified reflexive thought (Ong, 1988; Giddens, 1990). As moderns acted on positions as different as Luther's Protestantism and the science of Descartes and Newton, they would reflect on the results, eventually undermining many of these ideas. As a result, a strong vein of irony runs through the modern period.

In manufacturing, Western Europe's great strides resulted from unleashing the potential of the machine. As Jean Gimpel notes[18], European use of machines helped create an "industrial revolution" in the 13th and 14th centuries, in such areas as agriculture, mining, and engineering. This appreciation of machines would later combine with borrowings from, and improvements on, China's machine technology. The list of borrowings ranges from iron plows to steel-making, belt drives to mechanical clocks, gunpowder and guns to flame throwers and rockets[21]. The very idea of the machine would become central to Western culture, combining with the grail quest myth to shape the new world story developed by Francis Bacon, Galileo, and Descartes.

Social experiments based on this foundational story were also well under way by 1500. Two seem critical. First, as noted above, the nation-state was emerging, most notably in England, France, Spain, and Holland. At first, these nation-states were economically less successful than Italian city-states such as Venice, Florence and Genoa, or those of the Hanseatic League. In time, they became the standard for ordering large societies in Modernity[19].

Second, sophisticated finance capitalism was emerging in the Italian city-states. For Wallerstein, and those who argue for European cultural superiority, Western capitalism and the economic world-system it generated is different because it offered "an alternative and more lucrative source of surplus appropriation...[than] collecting tribute"[4(16)]. Which seems accurate. Yet, capitalism also evolved as part of a full socio-cultural transformation, in which economic agents could act as quest knights. Western capitalism developed in a culture whose world story was in flux and, at the same time, had been exposed to the world economy managed first by the Mongols and then the Ottomans. As a result, it was free to evolve in directions that the successful world stories of the post-axial Ottoman and Chinese empires restricted. Similarly, the West improved Chinese technological innovation in ways impossible in the more mature culture. Finally, with emergence of the Protestant Ethic, capitalism would become "religious," as wealth became a sign of God's favor.

Negotiating the new world story

The evolution of Modernity's world story turned on a series of negotiations about how to reestablish order in a wealthier, more complex society. In each of these negotiations, people would interpret the grail quest stories to define and explore possible positions, act on the consensus, and respond to resulting events, refining their story. It's tempting to think about these encounters as "debates"[3] or characterize participants as radicals or protectors of the existing order[22]. From the perspective we've been developing, such approaches are accurate, but reduce a complex dynamic to simple opposition. We prefer to think of these encounters as experiments in Modernity's quest for order.

The first set of these negotiations appeared in the 1520s and '30s, particularly in the debate between the Renaissance and the Reformation, embodied in Erasmus and Martin Luther. Both opposed "clerical tyranny and corruption and promoted a simpler, more personal form of Christianity"[3(135)]. Both also encouraged individualism, secularism, and widespread education. They split over whether the quest knights of Catholic humanism or those of Protestant millenarianism should lead the reform of Christian society. For Erasmus, human beings had free will. As a result, educational reform was essential if those in charge were to bring order out of the chaos in society. By incorporating a reformed, essentially humanistic education into the Church itself, he hoped to address its corruption. Luther, on the other hand, insisted that an omnipotent God had predetermined everything. Human free will was impossible. In addition, Luther believed that the coming end of days made the reform Erasmus proposed purposeless. Erasmus feared that Luther's dogmatism would lead to a violent explosion in Christian Europe; Luther saw Erasmus' humanist individualism as the work of Satan.

Ironically, Luther's revolution would succeed because of the literacy caused by the education Erasmus proposed.

This disagreement was not merely "religious." Much of the conflict was political, reflecting the complex politics of Western Europe. Not only did it play out long-standing political differences and conflicts between secular rulers and the Pope[13]; it also became the platform for many of the major political confrontations of the time – Spanish vs. Austrian Habsburgs, French vs. Spanish, Spanish vs. Dutch, northern German principalities vs. Austrian Habsburgs[23]. In addition, this conflict was a product of the economic transformation that would flower into Western capitalism. Catholic humanism supported the feudal landowning hierarchy, and its ability to reform itself. Protestant millenarianism, on the other hand, supported the growing merchant class. That ideology would be most clearly stated in Calvin's Protestant Ethic. The successful entrepreneur became God's elect. Even before Luther and Calvin, the proto-Protestant rebellion embodied in Jan Hus in Bohemia at the beginning of the 15th century would occur in one of the key commercial centers of Late Medieval Europe. With the added transformative power of the printing press, the Protestant position of Luther and Calvin would become the early face of a capitalist social revolution[24].

Intensification of warfare

The Reformation position prevailed, and Europe lived through Luther's apocalyptic world story during a century and a half of war. The first of these "religious wars" was the Peasants' Rebellion of the 1520s, in which more than 100,000 impoverished Germans followed their "inspired" leader, Thomas Müntzer, who told them that true believers would be immune to musket balls[3]. The religious fervor of both sides intensified conflicts that were largely political, leading to a scale of slaughter like that in the Axial Age. In France, the Catholic powers slaughtered 70,000 Protestant Huguenots in the St. Bartholomew's Day Massacre of 1572. In 1588, Catholic Spain barely failed to conquer Protestant England with its Armada.

In this environment, William Shakespeare's tragedies served the same purposes as the tragedies of Aeschylus, Sophocles, and Euripides in axial Greece. He had lived through the ongoing antagonisms between Protestants and Catholics that had raged since Henry VIII turned the Church of England Protestant. These difficulties in stabilizing social order were reflected in his major political tragedies – *Hamlet*, *King Lear*, and *Macbeth* – written in the first few years of the 17th century. In all three, Shakespeare demonstrates the inadequacy of post-feudal monarchy, with its dependence on family lineages and the relationship between the king and his knights. As with Greek tragedy and its criticism of Homer's ideal of government, Shakespeare's work embodies Reiss'[25] moment of rupture when a new way of governing a more complex world must emerge. The birth of this new way would be as violent as the events to which Shakespeare was responding, and several of the leading states of the day approached the brink of collapse.

Jack Goldstone's *Revolution and Rebellion in the Early Modern World*[26] documents these breakdowns, which followed the re-population of areas all over Eurasia after the plague subsided about 1400. In England, population rose roughly from two million to five million between 1500 and 1650; in China, from about 100 million to about 140 million; in Asia Minor, population rose between

50% and 70%. These population increases would drive a cascade of other changes:

- Inflation accelerated – in England, for example, grain prices jumped 600 percent from about 1500-1640, while wages increased only 200 percent;
- Government tax policies were unable to keep up with inflation, as wealth came from activities not covered by older tax policies;
- Unable to collect sufficient taxes, governments invested less than needed in the public sector, and the wealthy started relying more on the private sector and were therefore less likely to support more taxes;
- The poor became poorer and the rich, richer – especially with the vast wealth of the Americas, including gold and silver – increasing discontent among large portions of the population;
- Increased population also meant more sons of the elite class looking for a relatively stable number of government positions, like the *shih* of axial China, resulting in more pointed competition among the elite;
- As a result of all of this, members of the elite class who were out of power used new initially non-political ideologies, such as Protestantism in Germany and Puritanism in England, to inflame the passions of the dispossessed, leading to social breakdown.

The result in Europe was the last of the religious wars – the Thirty Years' War (1618-1648) on the Continent and the English Civil War (1642-1651). As the religious fanaticism of people who were fighting for their salvation melded with political and economic ambition, the brutality became overwhelming. In May 1631, the Catholic League plundered Magdeburg in eastern Germany, and 25,000 Protestants were slaughtered. The city was set on fire, and children, thrown into the flames; and 53 women were beheaded in the church where they sought refuge[3(129)]. While the killing wasn't as widespread and disturbing in England, the combination of regicide and the devastation of a decade of civil war ratcheted the fear of chaos to the levels experienced in Greece during the 5th century BCE and China during the 4th century BCE.

As Goldstone[26] emphasizes, similar social breakdowns were occurring in post-axial states. In the Ottoman Empire, army revolts from 1589 to 1648 brought the empire to the verge of collapse; in China, the crises that began in 1590 would result in the fall of the Ming in 1644. The responses to the breakdowns in early modern Europe and the post-axial states differed in an important way: While the post-axial states re-imposed order by returning to the institutions and behaviors grounded in their traditional world stories, the early modern Europeans, especially the English, would move toward a new way of experiencing the world and governing society. Theodore Rabb even suggests that the response to these events marks the period of most intense change in the emergence of modern Europe: Between "the early 1630s and the early 1670s ... there was a change in direction more dramatic and decisive than any that occurred in a forty-year period between the beginnings of the Reformation and the French Revolution"[27(3-4)].

The new world story

As devastating as they were, those wars also reflected the enormous energies liberated in the process of cultural transformation. By 1650, the center of Western capitalism had shifted from the Italian city-states to Holland, where the Amsterdam Bourse and Dutch merchant class were able to take advantage of the gold the Spanish had plundered from the Americas to increase world trade[19]. These English, French and Dutch quest knights were building international networks, whether in settling North America or establishing trading settlements in coastal areas of Africa, India, and Indonesia. This energy would also spill into the creation of the modern era's new world story.

At its heart, that story would have to address the devastation and chaos of recent wars, just as the axial Chinese and Greeks had. Alfred Crosby calls it "a yearning, a demand, for order"[28(10)]. Luther's God had been willful and unknowable. In response, European thinkers would create Science, the story of a rational world that could be understood through reason. The belief/worship system of Christianity would become a matter of private choice among "competing ways to salvation"[29(86)], dividing life into clearly marked secular and sacred spheres.

Yet, in spite of the rise of secularism, the quest to bring God's perfected world to Earth would continue at the center of the negotiation of Modernity's world story. The conflict here is not between the religious and the anti-religious, but between different ways of acting on the religious spirit[30,31]. The negotiations concerning how to do so would now continue in the confrontation between René Descartes and Thomas Hobbes over the nature of the science at the heart of the new world story text.

By the mid-17th century, a rich context already existed for their conversation about the purpose of science. Francis Bacon (1561-1626) had called for an experimental science that could "discover the hidden powers by which nature moves in order to gain mastery over it," relying on the work of the "priestlike" scientist[3(39)]. Bacon remained a theoretician; others, such as Galileo Galilee (1564-1642), were laying the practical foundations for modern science. Galileo would help fix two important ideas at its heart. First, the universe is a "grand book ... which stands continually open to our gaze ... written in the language of mathematics" (Galileo, as quoted in [10(283)]). While the senses distort, mathematics would allow people to rightly read nature's book: "If the ears, the tongue, and the nostrils were taken away, the figures, the numbers, and the motions would indeed remain, but not the odors nor the tastes nor the sounds" (Galileo, as quoted in [32(94)]). Second, this underlying "true" world was to be understood as a machine, Kepler's "machine of the universe ... similar to a clock" (Kepler, as quoted in [17(33)]), a universe of "dead" matter in which living things, especially human intelligence, are a special case.

For the most part, Descartes and Hobbes agreed. Both believed in the Christian God, but had been terrified by the excesses of religious fanaticism; both agreed that the senses distort the world; both wished to use Galileo's mathematics as a new path to truth; both believed that science could enable human beings to master nature and build a more humane, prosperous society[3]. Their fundamental differences about the nature of science were grounded in different understandings of how well it is possible to know God's world.

For Descartes (1596-1650), science was the search for the Truth, which would enable scientists to "discover the ground for a radical transformation of European society"[3(177)]. Through the sort of experiments that Bacon had championed, Descartes wanted to strip the distortions that the senses created in order to penetrate the underlying reality. With such a science, one could "believe only what is perfectly known and inescapable of being doubted," producing the certainty that "proceeds solely from the light of reason" (Descartes, as quoted in [3(191)]). Such a science of certainty, with the potential to remake the world, was possible, he believed, for two reasons. First, the human being alone of all living things is not merely composed of passive matter (*res extensa*) but is also a thinking being (*res cognitans*). As a result, human beings have the godlike ability to remake the world so that it is "no longer a cosmos or a creation independent of man but a human artifact"[3(200)]. Second, science can be true because mathematics, as the language of the universe, is true, and, Descartes believed, God is not a deceiver.

For Hobbes (1588-1679), science was not the search for the Truth, which he thought ultimately unknowable, but for knowledge of how things worked. Because our perceptions did not provide a trustworthy representation of the underlying reality, science must study the dynamics by which an omnipotent God willed motion to occur. Human beings can never know the truth of these dynamics with certainty, only that a specific explanation works, enabling people to manipulate parts of the world. Human beings were not, as Descartes believed, thinking things, but subject to the same laws of motion that God wills for all other things. Moreover, because God is omnipotent, Descartes' reliance on finding the truth was misplaced; God could deceive us[3].

In a society exhausted by a century and a half of warfare, Descartes's vision must have seemed vastly superior, offering a way to realize the dream of rational order. In contrast to the medieval worldview, Descartes' rational God had created a knowable order, ruled by universal laws that human beings could understand and take advantage of. Chaos had prevailed only because people had not properly exercised their rational powers. Now, the *viri spirituales* would no longer be medieval monks, preparing God's perfect kingdom on Earth; rather, they would be scientific quest knights leading the march "toward ever greater perfection of human nature"[33(5)], progressively learning God's laws and applying them to society. This story was already being enacted in the flurry of scientific activity, including that of:

- Robert Boyle, whose physics led him to describe "experimental research as a kind of worship"[17(153)];

- William Harvey, who discovered the circulation of the blood;
- Antoni van Leeuwenhoek, who first viewed micro-organisms through a microscope;
- Isaac Newton, whose mechanical physics finished the modern world story much as Aristotle's work had finished the axial Greek world story.

In many ways, Descartes and Newton were Modernity's Plato and Aristotle, crystallizing the new world story. According to that story, the world consists of distinct "things" that obey universal, unchanging laws of motion, much like the particles in a physics experiment. As things interact according to those laws, they create a pattern of linear cause-and-effect. If you could know the position of all things and the laws they followed, you could also know how everything would develop. To put it in religious terms, you could see God's plan for the world as it unfolded according to His laws. Science was mankind's vehicle for decoding the book of nature and understanding God's plan, which was both deterministic and teleological. With that understanding, people could recreate the world and master the chaos.

Enlightenment commentary

From the approach developed in this book, the Enlightenment was a sprawling series of explorations – ranging from how to gather scientific knowledge and apply it as technology, to how to search for "a rational vindication of morality"[34(50)] or govern complex societies in a world stripped of religious certainty. And with the printing press and widespread literacy, it became possible to think and say almost anything. As David Hume (1711-1776) characterized the times, quoting Tacitus, "Rare the happiness of times, when it is licit to think what you like and to say what you think" (as quoted in 35(152)). In its attack on "the prejudices of which the human race has so long been victim," to use d'Holbach's words (as quoted in 35(15)), Enlightenment thinkers left no holy of holies untouched.

The best-known critic of establishment Christianity is probably Baruch Spinoza (1632-77). But even before his infamous attacks, the Diggers, Levelers and Ranters of the English Civil War were reinterpreting Christianity just as radically. Gerard Winstanley (1609-1676), for example, insisted in the 1650s, "The whole creation ... is the clothing of God." He also warned that "the old kingly clergy ... are continually distilling their blind principles in the people, and do thereby nurse up ignorance in them" (as quoted in 36(112-13)). Like Winstanley, Spinoza analyzed the Bible as a human text, equated God with nature, and denounced the Church for appealing to the superstition of the masses. He also insisted that a free press and democracy actually strengthened the state.

Pierre Bayle outraged much of Europe when he wrote in the early 1680s that "atheism does not necessarily lead to the corruption of morals" (as quoted in 35(120-1)), and Julien Offray de la Mettrie explained that only a society of atheists could be virtuous. On the other hand, Gottfried Wilhelm Leibniz (1646-1716) would insist that God had made this "the best of all possible worlds," the position Voltaire (1694-1778) ridiculed in *Candide*.

While many Enlightenment thinkers criticized organized religion, several found God substitutes. Adam Smith (1723-1793), Anne-Robert-Jacques Turgot (1727-1781), and Cesare Beccaria (1738-1794) found God in the forces that drove economic activity. Here, they insisted that "society will progress and improve if the laws of the market are set free and left untrammeled"[22(107)]. Smith's "Invisible Hand," especially, suggests a protecting Providence, if we only "worship" it properly[35]. In their works, they defined the free market economics that became central to the modern world story.

From a different perspective, Giambattista Vico (1668-1744) saw Providence in the unfolding of history. In his *New Science*, published in 1725, Vico pictured history as an inexorably linear progress through a number of stages. The highest of these stages, people of the Enlightenment believed, was taking place in contemporary Europe. To define this stage Adam Ferguson (1723-1816) introduced the word "civilization", and humankind was soon divided into "civilized" and "non-civilized", "savage" peoples. By the late 18th century, Europeans had "discovered" most of the inhabited world and became convinced of their cultural superiority. While this Eurocentrism had roots in pre-modern European culture[37,38], the Enlightenment's linear, progressive view of the world, in the writings of Vico and Ferguson, Turgot, Voltaire, and Condorcet (1743-1794), stated it most forcefully.

This kind of sprawling intellectual exploration also appeared in the Enlightenment thinkers who sought to understand what it means to be human. Hobbes, in *Leviathan*, and Hugo Grotius (1583-1645), in *On the Law of War and Peace*, saw the human common denominator in fear. What allows people to form society, and thus to give up their personal freedom, both agreed, was Hobbes' "war of all on all" "in the state of nature." And so, their mutual fear drove people to congregate and give sovereignty to a power that would protect them[35].

John Locke (1632-1704) agreed that society was a contract that its members agreed to and saw its institutions as the great bulk wards of order. Locke believed, however, that this contract was largely about protecting property and that its members had the right to periodically reevaluate it. Denis Diderot (1713-1784) took Locke's call for periodic reevaluation to its logical end, calling for the downtrodden to rise against their oppressors[22]. Others viewed the position of Hobbes and Grotius as far too limited. Smith, in *The Theory of Moral Sentiment*, suggests that it was not fear or reason that united men, but sympathy through the exercise of imagination. Similarly, Jean-Jacques Rousseau (1712-1778) viewed pity as the emotion that bound humans together. And Hume wrote, in his *Treatise on Human Nature*, that reason ought to be "the slave of passions and can never pretend to any other office but to serve and obey them" (as quoted in[35(94)]).

This is only a sampling of the many positions early Enlightenment thinkers took, running the gamut from the conservatism of Voltaire and Frederick the Great (1712-1786) to the radicalism of Diderot and Thomas Paine (1737-1809). Our point is that these thinkers offered their culture a diverse stew of approaches to creating a Western model for an ordered society, all open to incorporation into the still-evolving modern world story.

Throughout most of the 18th century, establishment-oriented Enlightenment thinkers were most influential, just as the propertied interests "won" the English Civil War[36]. As Israel notes, the world seemed to be improving, and even radical thinkers such as England's Richard Price (1723-1791) wrote that the world had "been gradually improving" and that "this progress must continue" (as quoted in [22(3)]). "Civilization" was perceived as an essentially moral phenomenon, and moral perfection was seen as the basis of technological and social progress. Then, another cycle of social breakdown seemed to throw Western Europe back into chaos[26].

By the 1770s, especially in France, population grew, real wages fell, and the country experienced a series of harvest failures[26(182)]. Unlike England, the French monarchy had been unchanged by the turmoil of the mid-17th century. Partly as a result, the economy changed much more quickly than shifts in government tax policy. It became clear that the free market policies of Smith and Turgot could not address the problems of rising poverty. A "widespread consciousness in influential circles of the need to abolish privilege and rank"[22(229)] began to emerge, along with a conservative reaction to it. A financial crisis overwhelmed the French monarchy in the late 1780s. By that time, Helvetius's call for universal education, Rousseau's liberal republican treatment of the theory of the social contract, and Diderot's urging that the downtrodden rise against their oppressors[22] became more and more attractive positions. Then, control of the National Assembly fell to those who believed that the monarchy could no longer serve the interests of proper order and social justice, precipitating the French Revolution.

The irony at the heart of the modern world story would now reassert itself. The French Revolution (1789-1799) emerged from the philosophy of those who, like d'Holbach, saw "philosophical reason as the only guide in human life"[22][20]. They wanted to replace Christianity with a Cult of Reason[39]. Yet, the resulting actions unleashed centuries of suppressed anger and frustration at the wealth and luxury of a nobility that had been unable to provide for the rest of the nation. And so, the Cult of Reason would lead to the Terror. At the same time, nationality was replacing religion as the basis of group identities[40]. Napoleon made the most of this shift. Marching under the banner of liberty, equality and fraternity, he proved that nationalism could produce wars every bit as devastating as religion had in the 16th and 17th centuries. The response of European power elites to this affront to the Enlightenment ideal was immediate, and even though the cycle of social breakdowns would continue into the revolts of the 1840s, the power elite could now reasonably argue that existing institutions were the best defense against chaos.

Meanwhile, people throughout Western Europe continued to act on the modern world story, producing industrial capitalism and political world domination. More and more, the scientific discoveries of Modernity's *viri spirituales* were being applied as technology – from steam engines to telegraphy, the spinning jenny to gas lighting and the gas turbine, modern steel to the electric battery. At the peak of the industrial revolution, between the mid-18th and mid-19th centuries, Great Britain became the greatest industrial/capitalist power of the world[19]. Great Britain, France and Spain were then fighting for the largest share of the New World; they were joined by Holland, which had been in Indonesia since the 17th century, and, later, Germany, for control of the Africa and Asia.

In acting out their world story, Western Europeans created one of the grimmest ironies of human history. The Age of Enlightenment, especially its highest flowering in the 18th century, was both the age of remaking the world in the attempt to build a secular Heaven on Earth, as Descartes and Hobbes had predicted, and of the European slave trade. This irony was clearest in the newly independent United States of America. In 1776, it became the first "state really limited to the profane goals"[41][(39)]. The new nation had also witnessed a transition from religious toleration to religious pluralism[42]. For most of human history, government and religious belief fused to ensure the "proper" relations between people and supernatural forces. Now, democracy, freed from its entanglement with religious belief, promised to serve society directly and immediately. Yet, the American experiment was largely built on slavery.

After the defeat of Napoleon in 1815, the European powers, with Imperial Britain in the lead, continued to remake the world. Europeans colonized Africa and India, and humiliated China in the Treaty of Nanking after the First Opium War (1839-42). At the same time, the technological recreation of the world accelerated. Plastic surgery, the stethoscope, and pasteurization; the sewing machine, refrigerator, and automobile; telegraph, telephone, and motion picture; revolver, machine gun, and dynamite – all these 19th century technologies emerged. Together, these developments demonstrated the power of the world story generated from the philosophy of Descartes and the physics of Newton.

It's tempting to think that the larger-than-life individuals – the Thomas Edisons, Alfred Nobels, and Louis Pasteurs – made this transformation of human life possible. Yet, they were only the most obvious movers of a transformation that required many complex networks of people, organizations, and material agents. From scientific laboratories to newspapers and governments, millions upon millions of decisions and interactions[43] contributed to remaking the world.

Much of Europe was industrialized during the late 18th and 19th centuries, and the self-reinforcing cycle of population growth, knowledge increase, technology innovation, and growing wealth accelerated. By 1900, London, Paris, and New York each had populations of more than three million, while, in 1800, only London had even one million[44(63)]. In the same period, world population rose rapidly, from less than one billion to more than 1.6 billion[8]. This kind of growth created major disruption and economic hardship, especially in growing cities. On one hand, larger cities meant more interaction between scientists and technologists and more innovation in theory and practice[45]. On the other, it created a wave of human suffering. Together these factors drove another cycle of commentary on the world story.

One key element in this commentary was the removal of the traditional God as creator-king, an effort to "undermine the credibility of God himself"[35(101)]. This effort had begun with the writings of Winstanley

75

and Spinoza in the 17th century. It continued in the 18th century, with Hume savaging the Christian God, the Deists' belief in a God who left humans to their own devices, and the various attacks of the French *philosophes*. By the beginning of the 19th century, science had joined the attack. Pierre-Simon de Laplace (1749-1827) theorized that the solar system had developed from a gas cloud and that the Universe was extremely old, far older than Bible literalists believed. In the 1830s, Charles Lyell (1797-1875) published his *Principles of Geology*, demonstrating that life had existed on Earth for millions of years. Then, Charles Darwin (1809-1882) theorized evolution in *On the Origin of Species by Means of Natural Selection*, finally offering an alternative to the Bible's creation story[46]. The traditional Christian God was no longer necessary to explain the world.

The questions these scientific discoveries excited would be complicated by the suffering in crowded cities and the treatment of industrial workers. The result was a to create a sprawling diversity of socially oriented commentary. In literature, it emerged in the novels of Charles Dickens (1812-1870); in sociology, in the works of Auguste Compte (1798-1857); and in philosophy, in the writings of Friedrich Nietzsche (1844-1900). Of these critics, the most significant were probably Karl Marx (1818-1883) and Friedrich Engels (1820-1895). In their efforts to reestablish social justice and equality in industrialized Europe, they attacked a power elite grounded in private property, but also created an almost-biblical mythology of "Historical Inevitability." That mythology pictured a fall from grace when egalitarianism faltered and evolved through oppressive agricultural and industrial societies.

Finally, the Armageddon of revolution would establish the kingdom of perfected Communist man, a 19th century analogue of the millenarianist apocalypse.

Then, during the first quarter of the 20th century, the irony at the heart of Modernity once again returned, to destroy its most important assumptions. The First World War (1914-1918) made it devastatingly clear that Enlightenment reason could not establish the perpetual peace of which Voltaire, for example, had written[35]. The technological progress that was supposed to continually improve people's lives had, instead, resulted in millions dead and a political morass that would continue to create chaos for another generation. The world seemed uncomfortably like the nightmares of conflict in Hobbes and Grotius, rather than the dream of reason in Condorcet or Turgot.

In addition, scientific quest knights were beginning to discover that the worldview of Descartes and Newton was fundamentally flawed. Over the course of the 20th century, one science after another has contributed to this reappraisal of how our world works. The Science 1.0 of Descartes and Newton would gradually be replaced by the Science 2.0 that followed the lead of Albert Einstein, Neils Bohr, and Werner Heisenberg, if the reader will allow us to make the distinction in such a manner. Among the most interesting of these developments:

- Einstein's theory of relativity suggested that matter was not "dead," as Descartes believed, but a special form of energy, continually in motion.

- Quantum physics added that the world was not as predictable or as open to being "decoded", as the earlier world story insisted. It also suggested that Newton's independent "things" were deeply interconnected and interdependent[47].

- Astronomy drew a picture of the universe that is both vast – with hundreds of billions of galaxies – and at least 13.5 billion years old.

- Neurobiologists now believe that what people see and hear is not a direct image, like a photo, of the world around us, as Descartes assumed, but the images that our brains unconsciously reconstruct for us, combining memory and sense impressions[48].

This is a long way from the world that Descartes and Newton believed in. The nature of science, itself, has shifted. With the older, Cartesian sciences, nature seemed a book filled with independent "things" that were to be decoded so that people could discover the truth. With the newer sciences, nature is a complex, multi-scaled nested network of phenomena – from atoms to molecules, organisms to ecosystems, and planets to galaxies. The job of the scientist is to interpret the signs those phenomena leave in order to create the best possible models[49,50]. Combined with the wars of the 20th century, this shift from the Newtonian Science 1.0 to the Einsteinian Science 2.0 destroyed Descartes's ideal of certainty in a controllable world.

Even the comfortable Eurocentrism of the modern era began to dissolve. In teaching literacy and numeracy to children in China and India, no matter how condescendingly, Westerners put them on the road to becoming equals. Science has become a global grail quest. Moreover, Westerners have learned that while they have advantages unique to their culture, so do Brazilians and Russians, Indians and Chinese. In today's global economy, we are all interconnected and interdependent. The world story Descartes so proudly articulated has finally consumed itself, and another version of our world story is emerging.

Empire?

Will some sort of empire emerge as the current period of cultural transformation comes to its close, as they did in axial Greece, India and China? A provocative question, well worth thinking about, but it may not be the most productive question. In both Greece and China, the Axial Age was a time of social experiment growing from – and limited by – each culture's foundational stories. In Greece, empire emerged as people learned that the political fragmentation built into its foundational texts made it impossible to meet the challenges of increasing social complexity. In China, empire confirmed the emphasis on political unity and social support, embedded in the foundational texts, enabling China to become the most consistently powerful and innovative society through most of the post-axial period.

From this point of view, the critical questions may be: What have moderns learned over the last 500 years? What must we do to meet the challenges of a fully global society? And what can we begin to do now to increase the chances of navigating this period in the most prosperous and peaceful manner?

For one thing, the emergence of Science 2.0 suggests a serious dilemma. Many of the most important social experiments of the last 500 years were grounded in Science 1.0. Yet many of the assumptions of Science 1.0 now seem mistaken. As a result, some of those experiments seem to be creating social dysfunctions as great as the challenges they successfully addressed. Consider three of the most important:

- Technology provided the ability to support billions of human beings at a level of affluence that was previously unimaginable. At the same time, the promise of Bacon and Descartes that science would let people master nature proved an illusion. Instead, it created a dependence on limited resources, despoiled ecosystems around the globe, and developed terrifying destructive powers.

- Western capitalism made it possible to create wealth on an unprecedented scale. Today, it has become possible to abolish poverty for a good part of the planet's seven-some billion human beings, although partially at the expense of the rest. Yet, that wealth has also created systemic corruption. All over the world, money seems to be the only thing everyone values; the media preaches that the good life is the life full of snazzy, expensive consumables; and governments everywhere seem to be increasingly corrupted by their relationship with the very wealthy.

- Nationalism enabled collectives of hundreds of millions of people to work together, mobilize enormous energies, and govern the most complex social organizations in human history. Yet the combination of nationalism with culture has defined people from other nations as the Other, to be feared and hated, or at least pitied as ignorant and a little crazy.

In the end, it is precisely these great accomplishments of Modernity that stand at the heart of the challenges noted in the introduction of this book. And, so, addressing these challenges will require the emergence of a new world story, grounded in Science 2.0, as well as decades of experiment.

We would like to conclude this book with some suggestions about what people in late Modernity can do to facilitate this process in a fully globalized world. However, before we make suggestions, it would be valuable to consider a couple of questions:

- How is the world story of Science 2.0 developing?
- What does that world story suggest about how human history is evolving?
- And how can we use that new understanding of human history in the effort to wrestle social order out these chaotic times?

To begin answering these questions, we turn back to a panoramic view of human history, as viewed through the lens of Science 2.0.

References

1. Huizinga, J. (1996). The Autumn of the Middle Ages, Payton, R.J. and Mammitzsch, U. (trans.), Chicago, IL: University of Chicago Press.

2. Tosone, A., ed. (2011). Accademia Gallery: The Official Guide, All of the Works, Florence, IT: Firenze Musei.

3. Gillespie, M.A. (2009). The Theological Origins of Modernity, Chicago, IL: University of Chicago Press.

4. Wallerstein, I. (2011). The Modern World-System I: Capitalist Agriculture and the Origin of the European World-Economy in the Sixteenth Century, with a New Prologue, Berkeley, CA: University of California Press.

5. Frank, A.G. (1998). ReORIENT: Global Economy in the Asian Age, Berkley, CA: University of California Press.

6. Jones, E. (2003). The European Miracle: Environments, Economies and Geopolitics in the History of Europe and Asia, 3rd ed., New York, NY: Cambridge University Press.

7. Morris, I. (2010). Why the West Rules – for Now: The Patterns of History, and What They Reveal about the Future, New York, NY: Farrar, Straus and Giroux.

8. Livi-Bacci, M. (1992). A Concise History of World Population, Ipsen, C. (trans.), Oxford, UK: Blackwell.

9. Abu-Lughod, J.L. (1989). Before European Hegemony: The World System A.D. 1250-1350, New York, NY: Oxford University Press.

10. Freely, J. (2012). Before Galileo: The Birth of Modern Science in Medieval Europe, New York, NY: Overlook Duckworth.

11. Ortega y Gasset, J. (1941). History as a System and Other Essays Toward a Philosophy of History, New York, NY: W.W. Norton and Co.

12. Bondarenko, D.M. and Korotayev, A.V. (2000). "Introduction," in D.M. Bondarenko and A.V. Korotayev (eds.), Civilizational Models of Politogenesis, Moscow: Center for Civilizational and Regional Studies Press, pp. 5-33.

13. Tierney, B. (1964). The Crisis of Church and State 1050-1300, Englewood Cliffs, NJ: Prentice-Hall.

14. Spengler, O. (1932). The Decline of the West, Atkinson, C.F. (trans.), London, UK: George Allen & Unwin.

15. Rubenstein, J. (2011). Armies of Heaven: The First Crusade and the Quest for Apocalypse, New York, NY: Basic Books.

16. Noble, D. (1999). The Religion of Technology: The Divinity of Man and the Spirit of Invention, New York, NY: Penguin Books.

17. Shapin, S. (1998). The Scientific Revolution, Chicago, IL: University of Chicago Press.

18. Gimpel, J. (1976). The Medieval Machine: The Industrial Revolution of the Middle Ages, New York, NY: Barnes & Noble.

19. Arrighi, G. (2010). The Long Twentieth Century: Money, Power and the Origins of our Times, New York, NY: Verso.

20. Eisenstein, E.L. (2005). The Printing Revolution in Early Modern Europe, 2nd ed., Cambridge, UK: Cambridge University Press.

21. Temple, R. (2007). The Genius of China: 3,000 Years of Science, Discovery and Invention, Rochester, VT: Inner Tradition.

22. Israel, J. (2010). A Revolution of the Mind: Radical Enlightenment and the Intellectual Origins of Modern Democracy, Princeton, NJ: Princeton University Press.

23. Wilson, P.H. (2009). The Thirty Years War: Europe's Tragedy, Cambridge, MA: The Belknap Press.

24. Wedgewood, C.V. (2005). The Thirty Years War, New York, NY: New York Review of Books.

25. Reiss, T.J. (1980). Tragedy and Truth: Studies in the Development of a Renaissance and Neoclassical Discourse, New Haven, CT: Yale University Press.

26. Goldstone, J. (1991). Revolution and Rebellion in the Early Modern World, Berkeley, CA: University of California Press.

27. Rabb, T.K. (1975). The Struggle for Stability in Early Modern Europe, New York, NY: Oxford University Press.

28. Crosby, A.W. (1997). The Measure of Reality: Quantification and Western Society, 1250-1600, Cambridge, UK: Cambridge University Press.

29. Nongbri, B. (2013). Before Religion: A History of a Modern Concept, New Haven, CT: Yale University Press.

30. Taylor, M.C. (2007). After God, Chicago, IL: University of Chicago Press.

31. Bondarenko, D.M. (2011). "The Second Axial Age and metamorphoses of religious consciousness in the Christian world," Journal of Globalization Studies, Vol. 2(1): 113-36.

32. Dolnick, E. (2011). The Clockwork Universe: Isaac Newton, the Royal Society and the Birth of the Modern World, New York, NY: HarperCollins.

33. Nisbet, R. (1980). History of the Idea of Progress, New York, NY: Basic Books.

34. McIntyre, A. (1984). After Virtue: A Study in Moral Theory, 2nd ed., Notre Dame, IN: University of Notre Dame Press.

35. Pagden, A. (2013). The Enlightenment and Why It Still Matters, New York, NY: Random House.

36. Hill, C. (1972). The World Turned Upside Down: Radical Ideas during the English Revolution, New York, NY: Viking.

37. Amin, S. (2009). Eurocentrism: Modernity, Religion, and Democracy, A Critique of Eurocentrism and Culturism, Moore, R. and Membrez, J. (trans.), 2nd ed., New York, NY: Monthly Review Press.

38. Lambropoulos, V. (1993). The Rise of Eurocentrism: Anatomy of Interpretation, Princeton, NJ: Princeton University Press.

39. Smiley, S.R. (1966). The Institutionalization of Revolutionary Religion from the Cult of Reason to the Cult of the Supreme Being, Madison, WI: University of Wisconsin Press.

40. Smith, A.D. (1993). National Identity, Reno, NV: University of Nevada Press.

41. Spieker, M. (2001). "Khristianstvo i svobodnoe konstitutsionnoe gosudarstvo" ["Christianity and the free constitutional state"], Voprosy Filosofii, Vol. 4: 38-46.

42. Beneke, C. (2006). Beyond Toleration: The Religious Origins of American Pluralism, New York, NY: Oxford University Press.

43. Latour, B. (1988). The Pasturization of France, Sheridan, A. and Law, J. (eds.), Cambridge, MA: The Belknap Press.

44. Modelski, G. (2003). World Cities, -3000 to 2000, Washington, DC: Faros 2000.

45. Spooner, B. (2013). "Investment and translocality: Recontextualizing the Baloch in Islamic and global history," http://crossroads-asia.de/fileadmin/user_upload/news/wp14_Spooner_Brian_Baloch_identities.pdf.

46. Pyne, L.V. and Pyne, S.J. (2012). The Last Lost World: Ice Ages, Human Origins, and the Invention of the Pleistocene, New York, NY: Viking.

47. Barad, K. (2007). Meeting the Universe Halfway: Quantum Physics and the Entanglement of Matter and Meaning, Durham, NC: Duke University Press.

48. Ramachandran, V.S. (2011). The Tell-Tale Brain: A Neuroscientist's Quest for What Makes Us Human, New York, NY: W.W. Norton & Co.

49. Gazzaniga, M.S. (2011). Who's in Charge? Free Will and the Science of the Brain, New York, NY: HarperCollins.

50. Hoffmeyer, J. (2008). Biosemiotics: An Examination into the Signs of Life and the Life of Signs, Favareau, D. (ed.), Scranton, PA: University of Scranton Press.

Chapter 3

Notes toward a Science 2.0 theory of human history

Introduction

One of the most surprising ideas our work for this book leads to is the power of a society's world story to shape its own history. How could a story such as Homer's *Iliad* help lead a society into events as important as the *poleis*' victory over the Persian Empire or the Peloponnesian War? If Science 2.0 can help us understand cultural evolution, a good place to begin is the way this emerging way of thinking about the world can explain the power of world stories. So we begin this chapter with one last, curiously specific example of how a society's world story can shape its history:

In *The Religion of Technology*[1], David Noble observes that four major 20th century technologies seem to fulfill what we've called Modernity's foundational stories, integrating the grail quest and the Apocalypse. In those technologies, the modern quest knights – scientists – provide the means to realize the millenarian vision of Joachim of Fiore:

- Atomic energy can deliver Armageddon;
- Space travel makes it possible for the elect to ascend to the heavens;
- Artificial intelligence can create eternal life, and;

- Genetic engineering allows for the perfection of the human race.

From the viewpoint we've developed in this book, Noble's observation is no mere coincidence. Modernity's world story evolved from the 12th century millenarianism and the grail quest mythology, through the world story shaped by thinkers such as Bacon, Galileo, and Descartes, to the story that created a world where technology is essential. Certainly, the history of the last 500 years is much more than the inevitable fulfillment of 12th century stories. Yet, these stories seem to have had a powerful shaping influence.

Is it possible that stories written at the end of the 12th century evolved to guide the actions and discoveries of the most well educated people of the 20th century, *most of whom have never even read those stories*? In answering the question, this chapter explores a way of thinking about cultural evolution in the light of Science 2.0, with an eye toward what that means for the transformational period we are living through today.

The world story of Science 2.0 is still emerging. So there's no way to know exactly how it will develop. Still five of its most important elements already seem clear:

- First, our universe is very, very old. Every phenomenon happening today is assumed to stem from the Big Bang, more than 13.5 billion years ago, and is linked in a single process.

- Second, Einstein's $E=mc^2$ suggests that every "thing" around us is a form of energy, structured in a network of networks – from sub-atomic particles in atoms to galaxies in the Universe as a whole. As a result, almost every phenomenon is networked, on a variety of scales, to many, many others. (See description of networks below.)

- Third, everything around us is constantly changing. That change began with the Big Bang and continues today, from sub-atomic particles blinking in and out of existence, to molecules mutating in DNA, and global warming. Moreover, agents in networks at many scales can create cascades of change. So, a few genes mutating in Chinese fowl around 1916 resulted in a flu epidemic that killed millions during and after World War I.

- Fourth, our brains give the impression that we are directly experiencing the world as it *actually* is. That's an illusion. Our eyes, for example, do not provide photographic images. They send hundreds of thousands of tiny points of perception that our brains combine with memories. In this way, the brain constructs images so that we can interpret a world we can only see indirectly. We only perceive what the brains tells us is there, and that is sometimes inaccurate[2,3].

- Finally, the scientist is not a searcher for the truth, as Descartes assumed. Rather, because people can only *interpret* the world, the scientist looks for the best possible model/story to explain any phenomenon. Some of those models become what Thomas Kuhn calls a "paradigm," and other scientists in the field use it to structure their work. The movement from Science 1.0 to Science 2.0 is just such a paradigm/model/story shift.

On networks

Because networks are essential for understanding Science 2.0, it's worth taking a quick look at their nature before going on. Science 1.0 demands that we think in terms of independent "things," including people, each of which has its individual identity. Science 2.0 invites us to think in terms of networks and the agents that make them up. (Much has been written about networks. For the curious reader, we recommend Bruno Latour's ideas about Actor-Network Theory[4,5].)

An agent is any "actant" whose behavior can cause a response in other agents. In the struggle to thrive in the world of Science 2.0, agents will try to enlist other agents into networks. In biological networks, living things can enlist: members of their species, as in a herd of zebras; other species, as with the bacteria that live in the human stomach and help people digest their food; and "technological" assistance, as in the dams that beavers build.

In cultural networks, humans enlist: other people; other species, as with domesticated animals; stories, in the expanded sense we've been using; technology; and social institutions. What makes stories, technology, and institutions "actants" is their ability to change the behavior of other agents in the network[5]. After all, people started to live very differently when cars became affordable, and the Internet has made a thoroughly globalized world a reality.

Such networks are continually changing, as agents join, leave, or remain members. Not only that. As agents change individually, they can create cascades of change among other network members, who depend on them. World War I, for instance, was fought by two competing networks, the Allies and the Central Powers. The war's outcome was largely determined by changes in these networks. In 1917, the United States joined the Allies and, then, Russia withdrew. One of the most important events determining the result was the introduction to the Allied network in 1917 of a new technological agent, the tank.

In short, networks provide the flexible structure that living systems need to evolve. These networks enable agents to connect or disconnect, as their environments shift; they also provide the constraint that enables very different agents to work together.

In the world of Science 2.0, everything is changing, the unpredictable happens frequently, and living things can perceive such change only indirectly. In such a world, how can anything as fragile as a bacterium, a flower or a human being thrive? The answer, we argue, is evolution.

Evolution 2.0

Like science in general, evolution has been going through a paradigm shift in recent decades. The older paradigm is the neo-Darwinian "modern synthesis," which emerged in the 1940s. This model of evolution combined Darwin's natural selection with the study of genetics[6].

Neo-Darwinian evolution has three key qualities. First, as a process, it is gradual, driven by small changes that result from purely random, undirected mutations of the genes. Second, physical form, as well as much behavior, is the automatic product of genes. In this way, DNA can be compared to a recipe, "a set of *instructions* which, if obeyed in the right order, will result in a cake"(author's italics)[7(419)]. Third, the living products of their DNA instructions are then tested for fitness through "natural selection," their interactions with other living things and the forces of nature in their environments. With neo-Darwinian theory, "the history of life at all levels – including and even beyond the level of speciation and species extinction events, embracing all macroevolutionary phenomena – is fully accounted for by the processes that operate with populations and species"[8(39)].

As a result of these qualities, neo-Darwinism presents living things as relatively passive – more acted upon than acting – in the process of evolution. At the smallest scale, the "micro-scale," living things must obey their DNA's instructions; organisms are the "vehicles" that carry their "replicator" genes[9]. On the largest scale, the "macro-scale," they are subject to the forces of natural selection. Some living things can learn and change their behavior. But evolution and learning are distinct processes.

Not all students of evolution agreed with this gene-centered model. In the 1960s, Dmitry Belyaev noticed that stressful environments could activate normally inactive genes, and provoke significant changes. Similarly, C.H. Waddington discovered that genetic mutations would accumulate during periods when the environment remained relatively stable. However, when the environment changed dramatically, those accumulated mutations would express themselves[10], sometimes in dramatic changes.

Some neo-Darwinians tried to incorporate such discoveries into their evolutionary theory[8]. But, by the 1990s, it was becoming clear that the modern synthesis did not account for the full richness of evolution.

The most controversial early challenge to neo-Darwinian theory appeared in 1972, with the idea of "punctuated equilibrium," published by paleontologists Niles Eldredge and Stephen Jay Gould[11]. They argued that macroevolutionary change, like the move from dinosaur- to mammal-dominated ecosystems, occurs in relatively sudden "punctuations" of normally gradual evolution. Ever since, neo-Darwinians have denied this rejection of pure evolutionary gradualism. More recently, work in fields such as molecular biology, biosemiotics, and modeling complex systems have made the neo-Darwinian model increasingly more difficult to accept. The new model doesn't have an accepted name yet.

So we'll refer to it as Evolution 2.0. (Because this is a short book, we present only a brief overview. For the curious reader, a much fuller discussion of this emerging paradigm appears in [10].)

This emerging understanding of evolution advances "a far richer and more sophisticated theory of evolution, where the gene is not the sole focus of natural selection"[10(2)]. Rather, Evolution 2.0 models the process by which life has come to explore what Stuart Kauffman[12] calls the "adjacent possible." In a world of constant change, even the most successful survival strategy can eventually lead to a dead end, as most of the dinosaurs discovered. Evolution 2.0 enables living things to explore new possibilities so that they can develop innovative survival strategies when their older, more established ones fail.

The key difference between neo-Darwinism and Evolution 2.0 is that the emerging model occurs in a nested network, where agency is spread *throughout the network*. As a result, phenomena from genes to cells, organisms to ecosystems, and even volcano eruptions or asteroid strikes, all contribute as agents in the evolutionary process. Moreover, because these agents are all interconnected, Evolution 2.0 seems like a much "thicker" process, a non-linear conversation between phenomena at every scale, rather than neo-Darwinian dictation. In this way, high levels of stress in the environment (macro-scale) can trigger "semi-directed" mutation (micro-scale) in living things (meso-scale), suppressing enzymes that usually limit such mutation[10]. This is not the blind and random change of neo-Darwinian theory. How a gene mutates is random, but chemical systems in the body encourage certain types of mutation to meet the challenge.

Learned behaviors can even be passed on under some conditions. Such behaviors range from preferences for certain foods, learned in the mother's womb, to songs that some birds and whales must learn. With these songs, dialects may differ, so that "members of a group are united by a dialect that is clearly different from those of other groups"[10(172)]. This sort of learning may be one of the origins of human culture. In these cases, the animals that inherit non-genetic characteristics may be able to survive better because of them. As a result, they may also experience genetic changes that strengthen those characteristics. Nisbett[13] goes so far as to suggest that the holistic and individualistic way of thinking of Chinese and Westerners, respectively, may, over the last 5,000 years have been genetically reinforced. The study of biosemiotics – how living things process information – offers insights into the mechanisms by which cultural habits can become the object of genetic selection[3].

With Evolution 2.0, we leave the world of Science 1.0, where most matter is dead and action occurs because of linear cause-and-effect. In the world of Science 2.0, phenomena at many scales behave as active agents. And because of their networked structure, and the communication between scales, evolutionary change can cascade in a non-linear way.

The pattern of evolving phenomena

Yet, even in a world of cascading, non-linear evolutionary change, most phenomena seem to evolve in a similar pattern. As the reader may recognize, that pattern – derived from the principles of complexity theory – resembles punctuated equilibrium, especially in the repetition of longer stable periods and shorter transformational periods.

Take a simple example: Put a chunk of ice in a pot on a hot stove. It will remain solid until it approaches its melting point; the molecular structure breaks down; then, it enters a turbulent "phase transition" and transforms into liquid. It will remain liquid until it approaches its boiling point, with a breakdown in molecular structure, becomes turbulent again, and transforms into gas. Phenomena like this alternate between the "stable states" in which their behavior conforms to established habits, and turbulent phase transitions, in which their agents explore the environment for behaviors that enable them to survive. The resulting dynamics can be

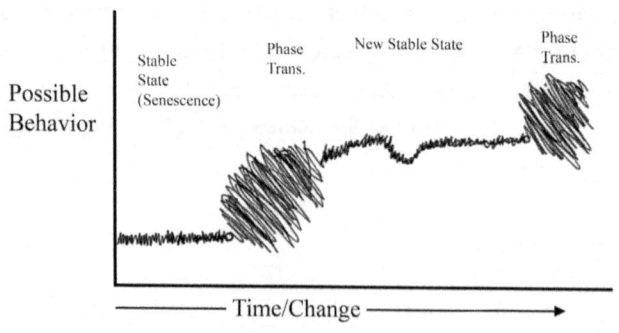

Fig. 1 *Pattern of evolving phenomena*

represented in the drawing below, created as a "back-of-the-cocktail-napkin" attempt to understand several phenomena studied in complexity theory[14]:

This pattern is overly neat and coherent, an approximation of the networks it maps, not a mathematical or literal representation. It is a guide for the interpretive explorer. As an example, consider what this model suggests about the evolution of mammals.

The earliest mammals appeared roughly 225 million years ago, a few million years after the dinosaurs appeared. As the dinosaurs came to dominate ecosystems across the world, mammals had to find niches where they could survive by avoiding dinosaur predators. Until the collapse of ecosystems, about 65 million years ago, mammals remained "mainly small, nocturnal, tree-dwelling creatures"[15(66)]. Yet, even though their body types would develop only in minor ways, mammals' genetic makeup continued to change through mutation at a fairly constant rate.

Most of those mutations would not be expressed in body changes until the 10 million-year phase transition, after the ecosystem collapse, during which those systems re-organized themselves. With so much constant mutation left unexpressed, "evolution of the whole [can proceed] without interruption in an obvious but imperceptible way"[16(7)]. This is a far cry from the neo-Darwinian "recipe" metaphor for DNA. Why did nearly 140 million years of genetic change in mammals only express itself fully in a phase transition if DNA is a recipe to be followed? Why are so many mutational "instructions" overlooked for so long, only to be exploited later?

The answer lies in the pattern in Fig. 1: Any complex phenomenon – from a molecule to an organism to an ecosystem – is a coherent network of agents, each of which is also a network of agents – atoms in molecules in cells in organs in organisms, and so forth. In phase transition, the coherent network that makes up the whole has dissolved, and its agents must experiment as they search for the physical structures and behaviors that will enable them to survive in new conditions. Here, long-accumulated genetic mutations can finally create major changes. As Jablonka and Lamb[10(272-276)] explain, this is precisely the sort of behavior that the emerging model of evolution suggests.

In the phase transition that follows collapse of the network, new forms of life – such as mammals – can flourish. As Stanley Salthe[17] notes, this is the most creative period of any phenomena's evolution, because of the freedom from the coherence imposed by older established habits. As they interact with others, the agents learn which new behaviors work. As a result, new "rules, laws, and structures" emerge within their networks[4(160)]. These become the stable-state habits that will continue as long as they are successful. Over time, the agents build relationships practicing these behaviors. The longer habits succeed, the deeper the relationships become, and the more the agents rely on their relationships. In this way, the networks of flora and fauna, predator and prey become stronger, habitual patterns develop, and agents begin to depend on those patterns for their welfare. These locked-in relationships and habits explain, for example, how mammals were ecologically trapped into such a narrow role for more than 100 million years.

At some point, the environment changes so much that behaviors needed to adapt fall outside what established habits allow. At this point, the phenomenon enters "senescence"[17], where agents struggle to meet challenges without going beyond those old patterns. Finally, environmental change becomes so great that agents can no longer survive unless they break out of those habits. The phenomenon's network collapses – just as the molecular structure of ice breaks down as it approaches its melting point – and, surviving agents, still connected in smaller networks, must either fall apart or reenter phase transition and develop another habitual pattern. Yet, living things have no way to anticipate what shifts may occur in an ecological phase transition. Evolution 2.0 suggests that, as a result, under-used mutations continue to emerge as part of the process of exploring the "adjacent possible." By thus creating possible alternatives, living things are preparing for the inevitable shifts, exploring alternatives they may have.

Given this understanding of evolution, DNA is less like a recipe than a "playbook." In games like basketball, teams may have certain frequently practiced "set" plays that enable them to make the most of their players' strengths. However, no one can be sure what plays the other team may be running. The game is too complex, and any specific game can develop in many different ways. As a result, each team has a book of plays from which its members work to adapt to developments that weren't expected, with tactics that have already been learned. In effect, each team is constantly exploring the game that is evolving, based on the playbook that gives them a limited number of effective tactics they can draw on. The game does not act out instructions; rather, it is a negotiation that players, as agents of their teams, informed by their playbooks, have with each other, and the other team, over the course of the game.

This is largely the way some researchers in molecular biology have come to think of DNA. For Jasper Hoffmeyer[3(111)] DNA is a "template" "used to recursively and adaptively re-create the system." That template records successful survival strategies that its organism may need. Some are currently in active use; others become available in times of change and stress. For an embryo developing from a single cell, the genetic template's "instructions" are activated in a complex conversation in which genes, cells, enzymes and the environment create complex feedback loops. All of them communicate so that the developing individual can prepare, from its very beginning, for the specific environment in which it will live. Each individual organism is a unique experiment, individualized from its species' shared template; each will also be tested by natural selection as it interacts in its ecosystem.

When ecosystems are in a stable state, this instructional conversation limits the experiments organisms make. The "purpose" of Evolution 2.0 is to enable living things to adapt so that they can thrive in the world of Science 2.0. So in the stable state, there is no need to explore the deepest possibilities of change in an organism's DNA. However, when ecosystems collapse, new survival strategies become necessary. As a result, over the 10 million years following that collapse of the dinosaur-dominated ecosystems, mammals experienced an "adaptive radiation," as "new teeth and body shapes evolved to allow exploitation of the earth's suddenly available treasures"[18(171)].

Our retelling of the story of mammals' emergence to dominance is oversimplified. Yet it makes clear the interconnected "thickness" of Evolution 2.0. Gould[11] points to this thickness when he discusses how evolution occurs at six scales – the gene, cell-lineage, organism, deme (local group), species, and clade (family of species). Hoffmeyer[3] develops the theme further when he explains how communications interconnects these scales. This thickness becomes still deeper as living things adapt to climate shifts, geological events such as continental drift, and even occasional cosmic events. Almost any of the changes in this network of phenomena may send cascades of adaptive change across ecosystems. Evolution 2.0, in all its thickness, is part of a worldview that Lee Smolin calls "relational": "Individuals exist, and they may be partly autonomous, but their possibilities are determined by the network of relationships. Individuals encounter and perceive one another through the links that connect them within the network, and the networks are dynamic and ever evolving"[19(xxviii)].

One last note: This understanding of evolution makes it clear why this process generally leads to increasingly complex phenomena[6]. In order to prepare living things to meet challenges they are still unaware of, evolution requires Kauffman's exploration of the adjacent possible. The process therefore continually produces and tests more and more diversity. And the progressive integration of such diversity is at the heart of increased complexity.

Cultural Evolution 2.0

Although Fig. 1 was created to explain physical phenomena, it also reflects many of the important cultural phenomena identified over the last half century:

- Michel Foucault's description of the 500 years of Western history as periods alternating cultural "continuity" and "discontinuity"[20];

- Gerhard Mensch's analysis of Western cycles of economic boom (stable state) and depression (phase transition)[21], and;

- Giovanni Arrighi's examination of the evolution of Western capitalism through periods of Italian, Dutch, British and American dominance[22].

Why do such different phenomena conform to this pattern? Because all phenomena that evolve seem to alternate between relatively long periods of relative stability and the shorter transformational periods, during which they re-organize their structures to

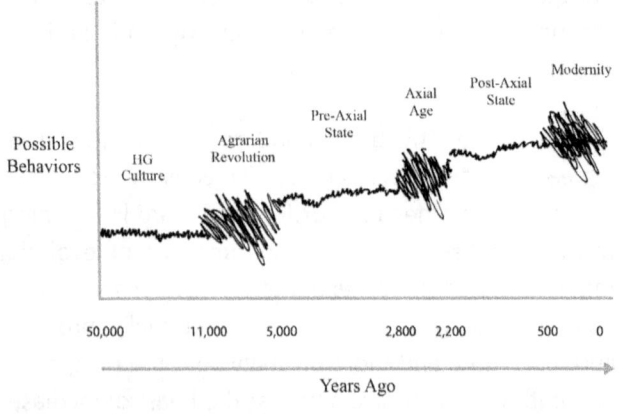

Fig. 2 *Human history as 'punctuated equilibria'*

meet changed environmental conditions. That pattern remains remarkably similar in both biological and cultural evolution.

From this point of view, a panorama of human history over the last 50,000 years might look something like this[23]:

History is too messy and abundant, and what we know with certainty too limited, to assume that events should conform to our abstractions; so we keep this figure imprecise. For example, the movement indicated in the figure is overly linear. Our date for the beginning of the Agrarian Revolution is 11,000 years ago, although 10,000 or 12,000 years ago would be equally acceptable. For the most part, cultural stable states do not simply end and phase transitions begin; rather, societies often move back and forth between the two, as anyone studying the halting attempts at lasting change in organizations, such as those in healthcare or education today, will note.

In spite of this intentional imprecision, our theory was recently validated by the more mathematically rigorous work of Korotayev and Grinin[24(34)], in their modeling of the growth of urban populations (see Fig. 3).

Here we see that urban population remains essentially flat in both the pre-axial and post-axial stable states, while it increases exponentially in both the Axial Age and Modernity transitions. According to Korotayev and Grinin, the main factor enabling such rapid population growth is an acceleration in technological innovation. As Brian Spooner[25] notes, this dynamic becomes a self-reinforcing cycle, because larger cities mean more people

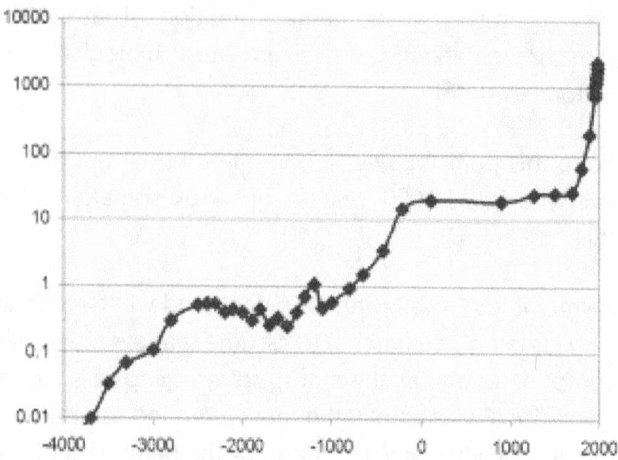

Fig. 3 *Dynamics of world urban population. In millions, for cities of more than 10,000 inhabitants, for the period 4000 BCE-1990 CE, on a logarithmic scale.*

exchanging and testing innovative ideas, creating more technologies that encourage still larger populations.

When you look at the last 50,000 years this way, human history alternates between three stable-state periods and three phase transitions:

- From about 50,000 years ago until the end of the Ice Age around 12,000 years ago, human beings were organized in hunter-gatherer bands of up to about 30 people and mega-bands of up to 200, constantly on the move, following the prey they hunted, very much like earlier hominids[30].

- In the centuries following the end of the Ice Age, population increased, people discovered agriculture, and experiments with new ways of organizing social life[26,27,28,29] emerged. This phase transition, the Agrarian Revolution, would continue to some time around 3000 BCE, when pre-axial states, such as Sumer and Egypt began to appear.

- These pre-axial states would continue to dominate human societies until perhaps 1200-1000 BCE, when increased population, technology and trade precipitated another cultural phase transition.
- The 600-year Axial Age enabled the cultures where it developed to re-organize themselves into bureaucratic empires, the post-axial model.
- The post-axial state would dominate human history from c. 200 BCE to 1500 CE, at which time further increases in population, technology and trade precipitated a second axial transformation.
- Today, we appear to be approaching the end of this cultural phase transition, Modernity.

As we noted in Chapter 1, there is nothing "inevitable" about this pattern. Societies undergo transformational periods such as the Axial Age or Modernity only when increased social complexity overwhelms their society-wide networks. The resulting breakdown makes it possible for the smaller networks within it to readjust, evolve, and reinvent themselves. Whole continents – Africa, Australia, both Americas – and significant parts of Europe remained untouched by Axial Age transformation. For example, Aztec and Maya societies never experienced such transformation. And those whose ancestors had been Aztec or Maya were swept up in Modernity only when the Spanish conquered them. *Cultural evolution, like biological evolution, is a matter of adaptation to specific events and conditions.*

Nor is it only the pattern of evolution that is similar in biological and cultural forms; it is also the underlying dynamics. With biological evolution, we looked at the emergence of mammals as an example of these dynamics. Let's turn now to a social analogue – the dynamics by which writing emerged as a powerful agent of cultural evolution. Sometime around 3000 BCE, the first "complete writing systems," which captured speech for the purpose of communication, appeared in Mesopotamia and Egypt[31]. These writing systems were essential to govern pre-axial states with populations of hundreds of thousands or millions. Until the Axial Age, writing would remain a tool of the people of power among whom it arose, priests, bureaucrats, and merchants.

During the 2000 years that followed the first writing systems, millions upon millions of social experiments increased the value of writing. It would be used for trade among empires, recording important stories, international politics, and even, in Egypt, as a powerful tool for political propaganda[32]. However, as the pre-axial cultural networks fell away in Greece and Israel, India and China, writing flourished as never before. Like mammals after the collapse of dinosaur-dominated ecosystems, millions upon millions of experiments became available to people in these societies searching for new survival strategies. In the Axial Age, writing became the preferred tool for communicating culture and storing knowledge, making science, philosophy, and the religions of the book possible[33]. In this way, writing moved from being a convenient way for people of power to keep track of growing wealth and make their orders known, in the pre-axial period, to the way for a much wider range of people to understand their world and help those throughout society adapt to an increasingly complex social world.

Note the remarkable similarities in the dynamics of biological and cultural evolution. Yes, the mechanisms are different. Where the template for biological evolution is DNA, any society's network of stories, especially its world story, serves the same purpose in cultural evolution. In both cases, the template stores historically tested strategies and tactics that have enabled their possessors to thrive. Both also make it possible to adapt by providing avenues for innovation that can be tested and, if successful, incorporated into the template. Note also that, as templates, both DNA and stories are passive[10]. Agents must act on them to create the interactions and eventually the habits of their ecosystems and social networks as wholes. They offer the range of survival strategies, the platform for innovations, and the limits that will one day threaten both ecosystems and societies. With this dynamic, biological entities enact their DNA and learn from the resulting behavior, while people in cultures enact their stories and learn from the results. These templates, then, have enabled life to thrive for 3.5 billion years, and a few human cultures to thrive for more than 50,000 years.

Finally, like biological evolution, the current understanding of cultural evolution is itself evolving. Until the middle of the 20th century, cultural evolutionists reflected the Enlightenment belief in progress. For them, human history was a journey from "lower," "primitive" cultures, often in the lands they colonized, to the "higher," "civilized" cultures, most obviously that of Western Europe. They generally defined that journey in terms of the deterministic workings of the universal laws of Science 1.0, ignoring human agency and cultural difference. John Stuart Mill insisted that this "preponderant" factor in "social progression" was "the speculative faculties of mankind"[34(585)]. For Karl Marx, it was economic factors; for James G. Frazer it was the thoughts of a few "superior minds"[35].

By the middle of the 20th century, evolutionists were taking the lead of Julian Steward[36], who began to focus on social evolution as a process of human adaptation for survival. They argued that different environments demanded different survival strategies. Cultural evolution, then, could be viewed as a process that enables people to take many different journeys to the same goal, through the same stages, but along many pathways. For much of the 20th century, those patterns/stages of cultural evolution – the best known is Elman Service's[37] progression of band, tribe, chiefdom, and state – were often treated as abstract categories, more real than the societies they described, in a process leading toward some ideal goal. By 1968, the complexity of cultural evolution was becoming clearer. So Service would write that no single factor could account for an invariable unfolding of cultural evolution. (For a full discussion of the evolution of cultural evolution till the end of the 20th century, see [35]).

By the beginning of the 21st century, Robert Carneiro was pointing out that "a process can have a *direction* without having a goal"(author's italics)[35(163)]. The emerging model of cultural evolution was becoming a general adaptive, essentially non-linear process[38,39]. As we've demonstrated in this book, even the movement toward increased cultural complexity[40,41] is more the result of people's adaptations to living in larger, more technologically advanced, and wealthier communities than a "direction." As with biological evolution, cultural evolution generally tends toward increased complexity because people are exploring the adjacent possible, diversifying the possible responses in their cultural template so that they can adapt to unexpected developments.

One reason this emerging model of cultural evolution can be so thick is that it is structured in nested networks. For Latour[5], social networks include humans, other living things, technologies, ideas and social institutions. For instance, this approach can help focus on the power of technology, in the auto or computer, for example, to accelerate the rate of change in Modernity. As a result of the cascading change at many cultural scales, every "interaction seems to *overflow* with elements which are already in the situation coming from some other *time*, some other *place*, and generated by some other *agency*"(author's italics)[5(166)]. Latour's idea of "overflow" is at the heart of our understanding of the thickness of cultural evolution.

Throughout this book, we have emphasized this thickness, as events unfold on three meta-scales:

- At the micro-scale, individual members of any society act on its stories, talk with others to better understand those stories, use the society's technology, and innovate on both the stories and technologies;

- At the meso-scale, these individuals become agents connected in social networks, ranging from families to states, and interact to drive the society, within the limits of their ecosystems, and its interactions with other societies;
- At the macro-scale, the interactions of different societies can generate a world system, as people in their social networks interact with their ecosystems, and both geological and climactic conditions, all of which shape and limit what they are able to do.

Cultural evolution occurs in the context of: events on all three meta-scales; the communications, interactions and responses they generate; and how they affect the ability of people in them to survive and thrive.

Moreover, events on all these scales are embedded in a history that one can trace back to:

- The spread of *Homo sapiens* across the planet, starting perhaps 70,000 years ago;
- The descend of our evolutionary ancestor, *Homo ergaster*, from the trees of the East African rain forests nearly two million years ago;
- The evolutionary separation of our ancestors from the rest of the great apes perhaps seven million years ago, or;
- The end of dinosaur dominance 65 million years ago.

At each step, our ancestors followed certain paths that limited what we human beings can do today, but also opened new possibilities. What happens at any point in history is the result of a highly complex network of networks, formed by millions of years of events on many scales, in which a change at any scale may have unforeseeable consequences that cascade through networks across the planet. This is what we mean by a thick conception of cultural evolution.

To illustrate, let's take a look at the richness of agents, structures, and other forces that would result in the Thirty Years War (1618-1648) in Central Europe. First of all, that conflict was embedded in hundreds of years of Church history, as well as the Church's interactions with governments across Europe[42]. This history includes the way the Church adopted the foundational texts of grail quest and the end of times, which it used in the Crusades[43]. When the Crusades failed, with the loss of Jerusalem in 1187, and the Church could not save people from the Black Death, it became possible that the job of *viri spirtuales* could fall outside the Church, as it would to the priesthood of science.

In addition, as ordinary Europeans became aware of the riches of Islam during the Crusades and, then, the expansion of the Mongols brought Europe into the first trans-Eurasian economic system in the 13th century[44], a wave of opportunities for trade and growing wealth followed. By the 14th century, world trade centers appeared throughout Europe, and the Church took advantage of the resulting wealth with indulgences, leading to the proto-Reformation responses of clerics such as John Wycliffe (c. 1320-1384) and Jan Hus (c. 1369-1415). The Thirty Years War might even have started about a century earlier, when the Hussite Wars

(1419-1436) began with the first Defenestration of Prague in 1419[45]. However, without the printing press, the Hussite Wars remained local. Perfecting earlier Chinese innovations, Guttenberg's printing press, however, made it possible to reach a wider audience with a Bible its members could read, as well as political propaganda[46]. The growing wealth of the Renaissance, as Europe recovered from the devastation of the Black Death of the mid-14th century, again highlighted the abuses of the Church, and Luther's response could now be communicated across Europe. The events that would then lead to the second Defenestration of Prague and the Thirty Years War even more fully demonstrate the thickness of cultural evolution.

Contributing factors ranged from the religious conflict of Protestants with Catholics to the political conflicts of the Austrian Habsburgs with the Holy Roman Empire, the Spanish with the French, English with Dutch; from the economic conflicts arising from the old landed class, which aligned primarily with the Catholic Church, and the new commercial class, which would align mostly with Protestants (eventually bringing us the Protestant Ethic) to technological innovations, especially the firepower of the guns and cannons, again borrowed from the Chinese. In addition, thousands of individuals would contribute significantly – religious figures from Hus to Luther, generals during the war from Mansfield to Wallenstein, a range of politicians including the Kings of Spain, Denmark and Sweden, and an army of merchants and manufacturers who made the war possible[47]. This is thick cultural evolution with a vengeance, causality spread out into every corner of society, all carried on a wave of social transformation.

Some implications

In such a short book, it's impossible to look at all the implications of this theory of thick cultural evolution. Still, a couple of them are worth examining briefly.

First, starting after the Ice Age, human history entered a self-reinforcing cycle of growing population, accelerating technological innovation, and growing wealth. As communities grew to thousands and then tens of thousands, wealth and power became more and more centralized in the hands of a few. For a species that had grown up in egalitarian bands, this inequality has continued to pose a difficult challenge – maintaining order in large groups while providing fair treatment. The challenge may even be more fundamental: Frans de Waal[48,49] suggests that the desire for being treated fairly is part of our primate heritage.

As a result, ideologies evolved to balance the wealth and power of the privileged few with their responsibility to maintain order and ensure justice. In ancient Egypt, this balance was articulated in *Ma'at*, the belief that the pharaoh was responsible for maintaining "right order," including protecting even the poorest from oppression[50]. It was similarly at the heart of the Biblical concept of kingship and the Chinese Mandate of Heaven. The desire for justice also seems critical to Goldstone's[51] dynamics of social rebellion in the modern world; only as the gap between wealthy and poor becomes extreme, and inflation makes it harder for the poor to buy their daily bread, do phenomena such as the French or Russian revolutions occur.

This balance is especially interesting in light of the breakdowns preceding both the Axial Age and Modernity. In the Eastern Mediterranean area, between 1200 and 1500 CE, for instance, the first "globalized economy"[32(102)] developed between partners in Egypt and Mesopotamia, the Aegean and the Fertile Crescent. Similarly, between 1200 and 1500 CE, the first pan-Eurasian world-system connected China, India, Islam and Europe. In both cases, population and interaction between members of different populations grew; new technology appeared; and the amount of wealth, along with those trying to take advantage of it, increased. In both cases, the majority of states in these areas had more and more difficulty maintaining order. In the pre-axial Eastern Mediterranean, all these changes contributed to the invasions often attributed to the "Sea Peoples" and the cultural collapse that led to a "dark age." In Europe, it led to the Protestant challenge of the Catholic Church, the rise of a new merchant class, and, combining these two with existing political tensions, 150 years of war. It also led to the world story that created a scientific worldview, capitalism, and the nation-state.

A second implication: Any society's network of stories, especially its world story, acts as a template for its cultural evolution, much as DNA acts as a template for organic evolution. As a template, these stories serve several functions. For one thing, they act as a storehouse for their society's historical survival strategies. In axial China, that storehouse emphasized the importance of political unity and submission to authority; in Greece, it insisted on the interplay of small, independent political units, where many members of the polity could express their thoughts; in modern Western Europe, it focused both on the role of the individual as quest knight/explorer and on the need for cooperation in the quest for salvation of society as a whole. In all three cases, these stories reflect a shared remembered past and suggest strategies for meeting the challenges of an unknown future.

These stories also form the basis for social experimentation that was so central to both the Axial Age and Modernity. Axial China's world story relies on the ideal of the sage king, who understands the *Dao* and can therefore respond to the world effortlessly. This ideal offers the basis for the schools of philosophy that sought to tutor China's axial kings, eventually leading to the combination of Confucian and Legalist thought that still dominates Chinese government. In Modernity, the world story was explicitly experimental, leading to quest-like forms in science, capitalist economics, and imperial nationalistic politics.

These stories serve one last function – to limit what is possible/permissible within their societies. As noted earlier, one of the key elements of all stories is that they have to leave out some details. Yet sometimes those omitted details can be essential for social success. That seems to be part of the reason for the differences that Goldstone[51] points out in different cultures' responses to the mid-17th century CE revolts in China and the Ottoman Empire, on one hand, and in England, on the other. The Chinese world story emphasized submission to ancestral precedent; the Ottoman world story, submission to Allah. The English world story focused on the journey of the quest knight. Largely as a result, China and the Ottoman Empire relied on traditional solutions and were unable to adapt to the greater social complexity that had helped create those revolts. England, however, was able to explore new solutions and moved forward to become a leader in the modern world.

In short, this combination of a basis for experimentation and limits to what we believe we can do that gives any society's world story the power to shape its history, as we point out in the beginning of this chapter.

All of which brings us to the third implication of our study: The world story of Modernity has reached its limits and requires re-examination and retelling for the human community to move ahead successfully. The most important experiments of the modern transformation – science, capitalism, and nationalism – are betraying their promise. And a new way of experiencing and acting in the world is essential. Far from being able to control nature, as Descartes hoped, science and technology have led us to the brink of poisoning our environment. And while capitalism has made it possible for a human population of more than seven billion, today, capitalism has replaced religion as one of the key elements of belief and a source of systemic corruption. In recent years, we have seen the reaction to that corruption in Egypt and Syria, in Ukraine and in many cities in China.

Finally, the cultures of nationalism now dominate most of the states of the world because those nationalistic cultures were so successful in organizing societies of hundreds of millions of people. Yet, with their insistence that "our" cultural stories are right and everyone else's are wrong, they are making it impossible to address the challenges Modernity has created. We live in a world that is globally integrated. Supply chains and financial networks can no longer be divided by state boundaries. Even information from all over the globe is now instantly available everywhere. It is no surprise, then, that the more important challenges people face today are equally global. Yet, as long as we are captive to our cultural stories, it will remain almost impossible to address those challenges. The old national cultures that were essential to building our complex societies now threaten to make us unable to solve the challenges that require international cooperation.

And so we will conclude with some observations on how our globalized world may be able overcome these cultural constraints and avoid the direst possibilities suggested in Huntington's[52] "clash of civilizations."

References

1. Noble, D. (1999). The Religion of Technology: The Divinity of Man and the Spirit of Invention. New York, NY: Penguin Books.

2. Powers, W.T. (1998). Making Sense of Behavior: The Meaning of Control, New Canaan, CT: Benchmark Publications.

3. Hoffmeyer, J. (2008). Biosemiotics: An Examination into the Signs of Life and the Life of Signs, Favareau, D. (ed.), Scranton, PA: University of Scranton Press.

4. Latour, B. (1988). The Pasturization of France, Sheridan, A. and Law, J. (eds.), Cambridge, MA: The Belknap Press.

5. Latour, B. (2005). Reassembling the Social: An Introduction to Actor-Network-Theory, Oxford, UK: Oxford University Press.

6. Depew, D.J. and Weber, B.H. (1995). Darwinism Evolving: Systems Dynamics and the Genealogy of Natural Selection, Cambridge, MA: The MIT Press.

7. Dawkins, R. (1987). The Blind Watchmaker: Why the Evidence of Evolution Reveals a Universe without Design, New York, NY: Norton Paperback.

8. Hoffman, A. (1989). Arguments on Evolution: A Paleontologist's Perspective, New York, NY: Oxford University Press.

9. Dawkins, R. (1976). The Selfish Gene, New York, NY: Oxford University Press.

10. Jablonka, E. and Lamb, M.J. (2005). Evolution in Four Dimensions: Genetic, Epigenetic, Behavioral, and Symbolic Variation in the History of Life, Cambridge, MA: The MIT Press.

11. Gould, S.J. (2002). The Structure of Evolutionary Theory, London, UK: The Belknap Press.

12. Kauffman, S.A. (2000). Investigations, Oxford, UK: Oxford University Press.

13. Nisbett, R. (2004). The Geography of Thought: How Asians and Westerners Think Differently... and Why, New York, NY: Free Press.

14. Baskin, K. (2008). "Storied spaces: The human equivalent of complex adaptive systems," Emergence: Coherence and Organization, Vol. 10 (2): 1-12.

15. Leakey, R. and Lewin, R. (1995). The Sixth Extinction: Patterns of Life and the Future of Humankind, New York, NY: Doubleday.

16. Jullien, F. (2011). The Silent Transformations, Fijalkowski, K. and Richardson, M. (trans.), London, UK: Seagull Books.

17. Salthe, S. (1993). Development and Evolution: Complexity and Change in Biology, Cambridge, MA: The MIT Press.

18. Ward, P. (1994). The End of Evolution: A Journey in Search of Clues to the Third Mass Extinction Facing Planet Earth, New York, NY: Bantam Books.

19. Smolin, L. (2013). Time Reborn: From the Crisis in Physics to the Future of the Universe, Boston, MA: Houghton Mifflin Harcourt.

20. Foucault, M. (1994). The Order of Things: An Archaeology of the Human Sciences, New York, NY: Vintage Books.

21. Mensch, G.O. (1979). Stalemate in Technology: Innovations Overcome the Depression, Cambridge, MA: Ballinger Publishing Co.

22. Arrighi, G. (2010). The Long Twentieth Century: Money, Power and the Origins of our Times, New York, NY: Verso.

23. Baskin, K. and Bondarenko, D.M. (2011). "Living through a second Axial Age: Notes in the time of an irreversible global cultural transformation," in I.I. Abylgaziev and I.V. Ilyin (eds.), Proceedings. Second International Scientific Congress "Globalistics-2011: Ways to Strategic Stability and the Problem of Global Governance", Vol. II. Moscow, RU: Lomonosov Moscow University Press, p. 130.

24. Korotayev, A.V. and Grinin, L.E. (2012). "Global organization and political development of the world system," in L.E. Grinin, I.V. Ilyin, and A.V. Korotayev (eds.), Globalistics and Globalization Studies, Volgograd: Uchitel, pp. 28-78.

25. Spooner, B. (2013). "Investment and translocality: Recontextualizing the Baloch in Islamic and global history", http://crossroads-asia.de/fileadmin/user_upload/news/wp14_Spooner_Brian_Baloch_identities.pdf.

26. Service, E.R. (1975). Origins of the State and Civilization: The Process of Cultural Evolution, New York, NY: W.W. Norton and Co.

27. Kuijt, I., ed. (2002). Life in Neolithic Farming Communities: Social Organization, Identity, and Differentiation, New York, NY: Kluwer Academic Publishers.

28. McCarter, S.F. (2007). Neolithic, New York, NY: Routledge.

29. Simmons, A.H. (2007). The Neolithic Revolution in the Near East: Transforming the Human Landscape, Tucson, AZ: The University of Arizona Press.

30. Fagan, B.M. (2004). People of the Earth: An Introduction to World Prehistory, 11th ed., Upper Saddle River, NJ: Pearson/Prentice Hall.

31. Fischer, S.R. (2001). A History of Writing, London, UK: Reaktion Books.

32. Cline, E.H. (2014). 1177 BC: The Year Civilization Collapsed, Princeton, NJ: Princeton University Press.

33. Assmann, J. (2012). "Cultural memory and the myth of the Axial Age," in R.N. Bellah and H. Joas (eds.), The Axial Age and Its Consequences, Cambridge, MA: The Belknap Press, pp. 366-407.

34. Mill, J.S. (1846). A System of Logic, Ratiocinative and Inductive; Being a Connected View of the Principles of Evidence and the Methods of Scientific Investigation, New York, NY: Harper and Brothers, Publishers.

35. Carneiro, R.L. (2003). Evolutionism in Cultural Anthropology: A Critical History, Boulder, CO: Westview Press.

36. Steward, J.H. (1949). Theory of Culture Change, Urbana, IL: University of Illinois Press.

37. Service, E.R. (1962). Primitive Social Organization: An Evolutionary Perspective, New York, NY: Random House.

38. Kradin, N.N., Korotayev, A.V., Bondarenko, D.M., de Munck, V., and Wason, P.K., eds. (2000). Alternatives of Social Evolution, Vladivostok, RU: Far Eastern Branch of the Russian Academy of Sciences Press.

39. Bondarenko, D.M., Grinin, L.E., and Korotayev, A.V. (2011). "Social evolution: Alternatives and variations (Introduction)," in L.E. Grinin, R.L. Carneiro, A.V. Korotayev, and F. Spier (eds.), Evolution: Cosmic, Biological, and Social, Volgograd, RU: Uchitel, pp. 215-54.

40. Christian, D. (2004). Maps of Time: An Introduction to Big History, Berkeley, CA: University of California Press.

41. Spier, F. (2011). Big History and the Future of Humanity, Malden, MA: Wiley-Blackwell.

42. Tierney, B. (1964). The Crisis of Church and State 1050-1300, Englewood Cliffs, NJ: Prentice-Hall.

43. Rubenstein, J. (2011). Armies of Heaven: The First Crusade and the Quest for Apocalypse, New York, NY: Basic Books.

44. Abu-Lughod, J.L. (1989). Before European Hegemony: The World System A.D. 1250-1350, New York, NY: Oxford University Press.

45. Turnbull, S. and McBride, A. (2004). The Hussite Wars 1419-36, Oxford, UK: Osprey Publishing.

46. Eisenstein, E.L. (2005). The Printing Revolution in Early Modern Europe, 2nd ed., Cambridge, UK: Cambridge University Press.

47. Wilson, P.H. (2009). The Thirty Years War: Europe's Tragedy, Cambridge, MA: The Belknap Press.

48. Waal, F. de (2009). Primates and Philosophers: How Morality Evolved, Princeton, NJ: Princeton University Press.

49. Waal, F. de (2013). The Bonobo and the Atheist: In Search of Humanism among the Primates, New York, NY: W.W. Norton & Co.

50. Assmann, J. (2011). Cultural Memory and Early Civilization: Writing, Remembrance, and Political Imagination, New York, NY: Cambridge University Press.

51. Goldstone, J. (1991). Revolution and Rebellion in the Early Modern World, Berkeley, CA: University of California Press.

52. Huntington, S.P. (1996). The Clash of Civilizations and the Remaking of World Order, New York, NY: Touchstone Books.

Chapter 4

Redefining otherness for the 21ˢᵗ century

Conclusion

Prediction is very difficult, especially about the future.

— Often attributed to Niels Bohr

And so, we come, at last, to the question we began with: What can people in the first quarter of the 21ˢᵗ century learn from comparing the Axial Age and Modernity?

Perhaps most significant, societies across the world continue to experience a jarring jump in social complexity and the challenges it brings. Growing populations and accelerated industrialization continue to increase global warming and industrial pollution. Resource, water, and food scarcities may also strike, no matter how clever technology becomes. And the availability of advanced weapons to groups with a grudge will continue to make international terrorism a threat. At the same time, intensive globalization – to a degree unique in human history – is making nations across the globe deeply interdependent. *And* billions of people can feel and see this interdependence when they access the Internet's truly worldwide web.

The challenges produced by this interdependence demand a level of international cooperation that doesn't yet seem possible. Some thinkers[1,2,3] predict a "world government." Others suggest a transformation to transnational government, where sovereign nation-states won't cede political independence, but will lose the thoroughgoing autonomy that makes them the "sacred cows" of international relations. In many ways, the inability of the international community to move effectively in that direction is the biggest story of the last hundred years. That story began with the failure to stop World War I, moved to the inability of the League of Nations to stop Hitler, and continues today as the United Nations cannot end the civil war in Syria.

Is there a lesson that this study can offer to a world that seems unable to develop the cooperation it so deeply needs? We think there is. And we want to end this book with some thoughts on what people across the globe can begin doing.

It's important to recognize how unsure the future that we face is. The community of nations can take any of many paths in the first quarter of this century. Cultural identity could combine with scarce resources to lead the world into the conflict suggested in Samuel Huntington's *The Clash of Civilizations and the Remaking of World Order*[4]. Or improved technology and international cooperation could result in abundance, as Peter Diamandis and Steven Kotler describe in their book, *Abundance: The Future is Better than You Think*[5]. Many other paths are possible.

We want to suggest actions that can improve the outcome, no matter what path unfolds. Those actions concern one of the key questions answered by world stories: What does it mean to be members of the group in which one forms an identity, and how should members treat other members and outsiders? Ever since modern humans emerged more than 50,000 years ago, these identity groups have provided the context in which all of us have come to understand who we are and how we should act. Every identity group – from the family to groups of friends, from organizations to nations – gives people the opportunity to learn in their interaction with other members of the group how they should act in any situation. Identity groups also let people know how to act toward those who are different – the Other.

In this way, identity groups are the keepers of the culture – the set of values, ideals, beliefs, behaviors, and attitudes that are characteristic of the particular community, whether a society, religion, organization or family. Such a culture enables people to create shared meaning, store it, and pass it from one generation to another through living networks of signs and symbols accepted throughout that community. Thus, culture defines how well meaning, trustworthy members of the community, behave. In such identity groups, people develop what Edward Hall calls a "cultural unconscious"[6(43)]. Among other things, this cultural unconscious defines the Other, whose peculiar behavior marks him as "slightly out of his mind, improperly brought up, irresponsible, psychopathic, politically motivated to a point beyond all redemption, or just plain inferior."

Such "peculiar" behavior may be as simple as whether a burp at the end of a meal is thanks to one's host or pure rudeness. It can also be as complex as the behavior that comes from the very different understandings of the idea of Law in China and the West. In either case, it can help define whether a person is worthy of trust and respect or fear and disdain.

One function of human history's periods of transformation has been to redefine identity groups and Others. During the Agrarian Revolution (c. 11,000-5,000 years ago), for example, human identity groups transformed from hunter-gatherer bands of perhaps 30 and mega-bands of about 200 to cities of tens of thousands and states of hundreds of thousands. Expanding the size of an identity group this way required a shift in human consciousness. People in hunter-gatherer bands know everyone in their identity groups. Anyone who is not immediately known therefore becomes Other and dangerous. To live in a pre-axial city of more than 10,000, on the other hand, people had to redefine what made up an identity group, expanding it far beyond those they knew. Similarly, to live in a post-axial city of 100,000 or a modern city of a million – or a modern nation of 100 million – the concept of identity group had to expand.

In the modern era, an important shift occurred in the way Western Europeans defined their identity groups. When the period began, religion was the major element establishing large-scale identity. People were Christian or Muslim or Jewish, and that defined who they were and what they were allowed to do or where they could live. However, after a century and a half of religious war, and especially the Thirty Years War, the dangers of defining group identity through religion became obvious. Religion then transformed into a matter of *personal* identity[7].

During this same century and a half, countries such as England, France, Spain and Holland were experimenting with national states. The feeling of nationalism that resulted from this experiment wove together ethnicity and a common language, shared history and the myth of a "homeland"[8], becoming the key factor of group identity, dividing people into "we" and "they." Between 1500 and 1800, the most successful states in Western Europe would be the nation-states.

As Western Europeans traveled the world, beginning in the 15th century, people in post-axial states, such as Qing China or the Ottoman Empire saw them as "barbarian" Others. By dismissing them this way, those societies underestimated the potential of Modernity. By the middle of the 19th century, however, these "barbarians" had humiliated the Chinese and begun their domination of the Ottomans. Over the next hundred years, these older societies would also redefine group identity in terms of national cultures, as did many societies of Central, Southern and Eastern Europe.

Most people living today live their lives in terms of their national identity. And even a hundred years ago, that seemed reasonable. After all, before 1914, the vast majority of people spent their lives in the cultures in which they grew up.

Not anymore. Walk out on the streets of Prague or Paris, Moscow or Philadelphia, Beijing or Buenos Aires, and you find yourself surrounded by a medley of cultures. Especially with the Internet, billions of people can learn what is happening almost anywhere in the world, sometimes instantly. They can also learn how people in other cultures behave. We have entered a world of cultural choice. For perhaps the first time in human history, most people can *choose* their identity groups.

As a result, people need to redefine the concept of identity groups. For one thing, with international travel and the Internet, almost anyone can see that people who are just as trustworthy as those of their own cultures have very different stories about how to live their lives. For another, in a world of challenges that demand international cooperation, people can no longer afford to see the Other as "irresponsible, psychopathic, politically motivated to a point beyond all redemption, or just plain inferior"[6]. For both reasons, *people throughout our globalized community of nations need to realize that the Other behaves differently because he or she lives with a different cultural story, not because of psychosis or malevolence.*

For the coauthors of this book, this is not a matter of creating a common, homogeneous global culture and abolishing the Other. Human cultures are deeply woven into all people's lives. Jablonka and Lamb even suggest that long-standing cultural habits can spill over into genetic change[9]. So we suggest another approach.

As noted in Chapter 1, human beings experience the world in terms of the network of stories that they accept. All of us need these stories to guide our behavior, and our brains are constructed so that, without conscious thought, we transform experience into coherent stories[10]. As long as people remain unaware of this fact, they remain slaves to their stories, because they assume that their stories *are* the realities they were created to explain. Mistaking a story for the reality it explains is exactly why Hall's cultural unconscious is so powerful.

Yet once people become aware that culture does depend on stories they have collaborated in creating, they can understand each other's behavior differently. My cultural stories and yours are different because they have different histories and offer different survival strategies. Yet your stories can be as valid for you as mine are for me. At this point, it becomes possible to discuss our differences, not as deviations from the One True Way, but as differing adaptations developed in different circumstances. Rather than surrender to Huntington's clash of civilizations, we can build a platform on which people from different cultures can examine how their differences interfere with communicating so that they can begin to address their common challenges.

As opposed to Huntington's clash of civilizations, this approach can allow people throughout the community of nations to begin building a "confederation" of civilizations. As they begin building such a confederation, they can test it, just as people have tested all the other social experiments of periods of historical transformation[11].

This effort can be part of the emerging world story that, for example, students of big history are beginning to tell[12,13]: The human race comes from a common origin, going back to the Big Bang. Our cultural differences enabled us to adapt to different circumstances. Those differences have helped us thrive in the arctic, desert, and jungle, the mountains and river valleys. Yet we share much from these common origins – from the majority of our DNA to our compulsion to transform events into coherent stories to our common heritage on this planet.

Such an effort may at first seem impossible. After all, it means that people must let go of the implication of enemy that has been built into the Other, which has existed as long as we have been fully human. Can we see the Other as someone like Us, who merely found a different story? Without such a redefinition, it seems unlikely that people from different cultures can come together with the degree of trust needed to address the challenges of our industrialized global world.

Fortunately, there is one model for building this type of cross-cultural trust. Until about 1500 BCE, Egyptians thought of themselves as the only island of order in a chaotic world[14]. Then, trade and political contact with the Minoan and Western Asian civilizations became more and more frequent. But how were the Egyptians to trust these "barbarian" peoples who had different gods and, so, could not swear on the Egyptian gods? Eventually, people form all these cultures noted that many of their gods were much more alike than they had realized. Egypt's Ra was like Mycenae's Apollo. Their "cultures might differ, but the gods remained the same everywhere"[14(55)]. Spurred by their need to be able to trust each other in their commercial dealings, they were able to create a platform for "translating" the names of the gods and, thereby, to trust that the Egyptian's swearing on Ra was almost identical to the Mycenaean's swearing on Apollo.

Today, the international community again needs to "translate" cultures so that we can establish trust. The

"Rosetta Stone" for this translation exists today in the study of stories, developing in fields from evolutionary anthropology to neurobiology and biosemiotics. Of course, learning to translate cultural stories is a much more difficult task than merely translating the names of gods. At the same time, the human community has so much more at stake. In fact, we face the very real possibility of creating the same kind of crises that led to the dark ages in the Eastern Mediterranean world three millennia ago. If we cannot overcome our habit of thinking in terms of the nation-state's absolute supremacy, it will be extremely difficult to address the challenges that threaten societies across the globe as they continue to become more and more highly technologized. And changing that habit of thought will require both accepting each other's cultural stories and transcending Modernity's "sacred cow" – the belief that the nation-state must be autonomous in international law and relations.

N.K. Sandars described the collapse of Mycenae, leading to those dark ages, as an "essentially artificial way of life . . . unable to take the strain" of a variety of natural and social pressures[15(197)]. Yet, how much more artificial is 21st century society? As Jose Ortega y Gasset notes, the collapse of a society so dependent on technology will not be like the fall of Mycenae, where most people could simply go back to subsistence farming[16]. Billions of people today depend on technology to survive. What will happen without the resources to operate our power plants, clean our water, and transport our food?

The stakes are, indeed, very high, well worth any effort in learning to understand and trust each Other. Even though we cannot predict our future, we must make the attempt, if not for ourselves, then for the sake of our children and grandchildren.

References

1. Tamir, Y. (2000). "Who's afraid of a global state?" in K. Goldman, U. Hannerz, and C. Westin (eds.), Nationalism and Internationalism in the Post-Cold War Era, London, UK: Routledge, pp. 244-67.

2. Wendt, A. (2003). "Why a world state is inevitable," European Journal of International Relations. Vol. 9(4): 491-542.

3. Carneiro, R.L. (2004). "The political unification of the world: whether, when and how – some speculations," Cross-Cultural Research. Vol. 38(2): 162-77.

4. Huntington, S.P. (1996). The Clash of Civilizations and the Remaking of World Order, New York, NY: Touchstone Books.

5. Diamandis, P.H. and Kotler, S. (2012). Abundance: The Future Is Better Than You Think, New York, NY: Free Press.

6. Hall, E.T. (1975). Beyond Culture, New York, NY: Anchor Books.

7. Nongbri, B. (2013). Before Religion: A History of a Modern Concept, New Haven, CT: Yale University Press.

8. Smith, A.D. (1993). National Identity, Reno, NV: University of Nevada Press.

9. Jablonka, E. and Lamb, M.J. (2005). Evolution in Four Dimensions: Genetic, Epigenetic, Behavioral, and Symbolic Variation in the History of Life, Cambridge, MA: The MIT Press.

10. Gazzaniga, M.S. (2011). Who's in Charge? Free Will and the Science of the Brain, New York, NY: HarperCollins.

11. Bondarenko, D.M. (2009). "The social world's parts and whole: Globalization and the future of some non-western cultures in the civilization and world-system theories perspectives," in J. Sheffield (ed.), Systemic Development: Local Solutions in a Global Environment, Litchfield Park, AZ: ISCE Publishing, pp. 17-24.

12. Christian, D. (2004). Maps of Time: An Introduction to Big History, Berkeley, CA: University of California Press.

13. Spier, F. (2011). Big History and the Future of Humanity, Malden, MA: Wiley-Blackwell.

14. Assmann, J. (2008). Of God and Gods: Egypt, Israel, and the Rise of Monotheism, Madison, WI: University of Wisconsin Press.

15. Sandars, N.K. (1978). The Sea Peoples: Warriors of the Ancient Mediterranean 1250-1150 BC, London, UK: Thames and Hudson.

16. Ortega y Gasset, J. (1941). History as a System and Other Essays Toward a Philosophy of History, New York, UK: W.W. Norton and Co.

www.ingramcontent.com/pod-product-compliance
Lightning Source LLC
La Vergne TN
LVHW020932090426
835512LV00020B/3321